On the Way . . .

*Short Stories and
Biblical Reflections on
Caring for a Loved One in Hospice*

Pam Northrup

Copyright © 2018 Pamela S. Northrup

All rights reserved. No part of this publication may be reproduced, distributed, or transmitted in any form or by any means, including photocopying, recording, or other electronic or mechanical methods, without the prior written permission of the publisher, except in the case of brief quotations embodied in reviews and certain other non-commercial uses permitted by copyright law.

Scripture quotations, unless otherwise noted, are from the New Revised Standard Version Bible, copyright ©1989 by the National Council of Churches of Christ in the United States of America. Used by permission. All rights reserved.

ISBN-13: 978-1-7335040-0-3

Cover design by Kevin Coppolino

This book is dedicated to the loving memory of my mom

Mary Hazel Odette Smith

December 8, 1942 – November 17, 2008

A Gift

Writing this book is a gift. It's something that I've wanted to do for many, many years. I think it took me so long because I wasn't yet in a place where I could tell the story. I needed time. Time to live with our experience, to gain some perspective, and to put our experience in the context of something bigger. Writing these stories and the biblical reflections has been a gift to me. It has enabled me to go back in time and to experience the journey with Mom again, this time as someone hovering over the scene rather than being deep within it. I feel closer to mom because I've been able to write her story, our story.

I write this book as a gift for my family and all those who loved and cared for mom. So many people were part of our journey. Some I've named in the book and others remain unnamed. Know that you were all essential companions in the journey. I have attempted to capture our experiences with the utmost integrity and sensitivity. I hope that as you read through these stories you will recall with affection the time you had with the person you called Mom, Grammy, Friend, Hazel.

I write this book as a gift to those who are currently caring for a loved one who is dying. When mom was first diagnosed, I looked for books that described how other families accompanied their loved one. To my surprise I couldn't find what I was looking for. I found lots of technical books written by professionals, but nothing written by a family member, from a family's perspective. I told myself that someday I'd write the book so that other families might find comfort, and maybe a little wisdom, in our experience. This is that book.

I write this book as a gift to those who are considering hospice care for themselves or their loved one. Even mentioning the word hospice can be unsettling. I know that first hand. In this book, I've tried to capture the blessing and gift that hospice can be to people who are facing life-limiting diseases and their families. I hope that this collection is helpful. I hope that this paves the way for more people to accept the care that hospice provides.

I write this book as a gift to professional and volunteer caregivers, to people working in the field of hospice, to pastors and doctors, and to others who accompany people who are sick, people who are dying, people who are grieving. This is one family's story. It's not intended to reflect anything more than that. Maybe, through our story you will gain insight into the patient and family experience in ways that you've not been able to do until now.

I write this book as a gift to anyone who wants to explore the intersection of life, death, and eternal life. Death is a natural component of living. It is the last chapter in our lives. The reality is that from the moment we are born, we are all moving toward death. This doesn't need to be scary. I hope that through these stories and biblical reflections, you will be reminded of your goodness, will see the blessings of a loving and supportive community, and will be embraced by the power of love, laughter, and peace as you are on the way in your own life.

There is one more gift. Visit www.onthewayliving.org to download a free Companion to this book. The Companion provides reflection questions and activities that will give you an opportunity to engage with the book on a personal level.

I hope that this book will be a gift for you in whatever way that you need it to be.

Pam

TABLE OF CONTENTS

Foreword	1
Prologue	5
A Word About Hospice Care	11
Part One: The Short Stories	**19**
Chapter 1: On the Way	21
Chapter 2: The Brain	29
Chapter 3: The Hospice Decision	37
Chapter 4: "I Want to Die Right Now!"	45
Chapter 5: Taking Care of Business	51
Excursus 1: Mom's Generosity Affects Everyone	61
Chapter 6: Surrounded by Love	65
Chapter 7: Nursing 101	69
Chapter 8: Managing Medications	77

Excursus 2: Mom's Reaction to a Surprise Birthday Party	85
Chapter 9: Hazel's Team	89
Chapter 10: Trip to the Beach	97
Chapter 11: The Talking Stick	103
Excursus 3: Mom Saved Me from Deadly Laundry	109
Chapter 12: The Branch	113
Chapter 13: The Shower	121
Chapter 14: A Visit from Daddy	131
Chapter 15: The Final Hours	137
Chapter 16: The Days After	143

Part Two: Biblical Reflections on Caring for a Loved One in Hospice — **151**

Reflection on 1 Corinthians 13:4-8, 13	153
Reflection on Colossians 3:12-14	159
Reflection on Ecclesiastes 3:1-8	163
Reflection on Ephesians 3:14-16	169
Reflection on Hebrews 12:1-3	173
Reflection on Isaiah 43:1-5a	179

Reflection on Mark 2:1-5	185
Reflection on Philippians 4:4-9	189
Reflection on Psalm 6	195
Reflection on Psalm 23	199
Reflection on Psalm 95:1-7	207
Reflection on Psalm 139:1-14	211
Reflection on Romans 5:6-11	217
Reflection on Romans 8:31-35, 37-39	221
Epilogue	225
Appreciation	233
For More Information about Hospice	237
About the Author	239

FOREWORD

When I first met Pam Northrup, she was at the very beginning of her seminary studies. Following her pastoral care mid-term examination, it was obvious that God had given her a gift for bringing clarity and faith into complex situations. Although she already had considerable academic ability, she continued to ask the very practical ministry question: "What does this look like in real life?" As she continued to challenge herself (and her professors) with this question, she began to integrate interpersonal insights and personal experience with her intellectual skills. Pam Northrup discovered for herself what her professors and mentors already knew; God has given her the heart of a pastor, and now hospice chaplain.

In this book, Chaplain Northrup demonstrates what it looks like and feels like to accompany her mother along the process of dying and into eternity. Here is the personal story of one who has been there with her

On the Way . . .

mother, family, and friends as well as now walking with others as they seek strength and guidance on the journey.

This is by no means a "one-size-fits-all, pie-in-the-sky, how-to-succeed" book. Neither is it a guide for avoiding the anxiety, tears, confusion, and faith challenges along the way. Instead, Chaplain Northrup helps us move beyond our comfort zones and invites us to join her on a holy journey. Initially, she provides clarifying information regarding hospice care; clarifying what hospice is and is not. For example, hospice is about offering a journey with a caring team of professionals, volunteers, and family. It is about working to alleviate as much pain as possible and providing as much control, dignity, and comfort as possible for the dying person and family. Hospice is not giving up or for cancer patients only. Hospice does not require a Do Not Resuscitate (DNR) order.

I particularly appreciate Chaplain Northrup sharing examples of her own everyday struggles. Readers will easily find similar concerns along their own journey. In my own life I have felt such things as the emerging of powerful emotions, exhaustion, and what to say or do when it seems like nothing helps. Faith struggles, laments, and doubts arise. She assures us that this is normal, even and maybe especially for religious folk.

We are invited into images and stories from her mother (it's about the one who is dying, not the rest of us) that will expand our own insights for help on the journey together. Examples such as "The Brain" for support system (Chapter 2); "The Talking Stick" for listening and understanding during chaos times (Chapter 11); and "The Branch" for sensing God's presence in the midst of doubt and helplessness (Chapter 12). Her mother's final days (Chapter 15) and the days after (Chapter 16) include powerful examples of faith, story, funeral, scripture, hymns, prayer, laughter and tears. Here is a fine example of Chaplain Northrup's seminary question "what does this journey look like in real life?".

The concluding biblical reflections and prayers are theologically sound and particularly helpful as Chaplain Northrup includes us into her own journey on the way with her mother. As we read through each text and reflection, we will see our own questions and stories emerging. As we wrestle with meaning and search for comfort, we will discover that we are not alone; that we are invited to walk on holy ground with the author and a great cloud of witnesses who share our journey on the way.

By sharing her own stories, Chaplain Northrup is inviting us to see our own stories through a new and

On the Way...

holy lens. She writes, "I've learned that when you expect God to be present, you are more likely to recognize that presence through the interactions and events of each day". (Epilogue) It happened for me. My prayer is that, on the way, you will also experience just where God is along this awesome journey.

The Reverend Tony Everett, Th.D
Professor of Pastoral Care, Retired
Lutheran Theological Southern Seminary

PROLOGUE

Walking with people who are facing life-limiting illnesses and death is a big part of my ministry. I've had opportunities to sit by the bedsides of many people, holding the hands of those who are on the brink of death, offering prayers and readings from the Bible. Being able to anoint the forehead of someone with oil and finding creative ways to share Holy Communion is a privilege for me and a blessing for others.

Along the way, I've learned that everyone walks this path differently. Some are willing to admit that they are dying more quickly than others. These people tend to be more accepting of the care and support that their pastor, family, and friends can provide. They're willing to speak openly with others about their pain, fears, and doubts. This openness provides precious moments for conversation about life, death, and matters of faith.

On the Way...

Because they are willing, their loved ones have the opportunity to journey with them. They can be intentional about being around their loved one. They can say what they need to say, and do what they need to do, for themselves and the one they love.

Others are less willing to acknowledge or accept their prognosis. They may seek life extending treatment longer than some or they may avoid sharing what is happening to them with anyone. Sometimes, it's because they don't want their loved ones to worry about them or feel sad. Other times, it's because they're not ready to say the words out loud.

Because of this lack of openness, unwillingness, or reluctance to face their situation, they are more likely to be isolated. They may try to carry their burden alone and miss the support of their loved ones. This causes their loved ones to miss the opportunity to share the journey with them and support them along the way.

I've found that the more willing a person is to share their illness and dying journey with others, the more care they receive and the more peaceful they are at the end of their life. This doesn't mean that saying "goodbye" will be easy—it won't be. However, because the experience is being shared with others, everyone benefits from being on the way together.

Traveling this road together provides opportunities to laugh and cry, to remember the past and speak about the future, to share thoughts and express feelings, to make apologies and extend forgiveness, so that the ones who are living and the one who is dying can support and care for one another.

Thankfully, my Mom wanted to talk about her disease and prognosis. She wanted everyone in her life to know what was happening to her and appreciated the support she received from friends and family. This was such a blessing to all of us who loved her.

This shared journey is holy ground (Exodus 3:1-5). It's the place where the presence of God breaks into our lives in real and tangible ways assuring us that we're not alone and enabling us to do what we might think is impossible. Moses was blessed to see God's presence in a burning bush, a sight which made it impossible to miss the power and presence of God.

There were days when God's presence was abundantly clear and other days when I wondered where God was in the midst of everything that was going on. The sleepless nights and the anxious days

On the Way . . .

narrowed my view of the world and sometimes made it difficult to see God.

It was on those days when I asked the WIGIAT question. WIGIAT is a made-up word that comes from the first letters in the question: Where Is God In All This? One of my seminary professors, Dr. Tony Everett, coined this phrase, this acronym that became a word, providing a lens for intentionally naming and claiming God's presence in every moment of our lives.

Asking WIGIAT reminded me to slow down and look for God in the ordinary actions of the hospice team who provided attentive care, the loving visits of friends and family, and the quiet moments when Mom and I just spent time together. God was present in the visitor who came bearing a yummy milkshake, in a bouquet of flowers that was delivered to the house, and in the phone call from a friend far away. Asking WIGIAT helped me see that God met us right in the middle of everything.

The stories in this book are true. They are glimpses into the funny, challenging, and poignant times of the journey we shared with Mom as she was on the way through death into eternal life. I share them with you in hope that they will inspire and comfort you. My greatest joy will come if in our stories you may see yourself, your loved one, and your stories in a new way.

Part Two of this book includes a collection of biblical reflections. The passages I chose are ones that were meaningful to Mom. They provided peace and comfort as she dealt with everything that was happening to her body while she waited for the promises of God to be fulfilled for her.

These same passages continue to influence my life and ministry. They shape how I understand who God is and how God meets us in the moments of our lives. These passages are among those that proclaim the powerful promises of God to meet us where we are and to love us completely as we are on the way in this life.

I pray that these stories and the biblical reflections will be meaningful to you. May they strengthen and comfort you, help you embrace the full range of emotions you may be experiencing, and give you peace.

On the way with you,
Pam
December 2018

A Word About Hospice Care

In my ministry, I've encouraged people with life-limiting illnesses, who are no longer seeking curative treatment, to consider enrolling in hospice. This is frequently met with confusion and resistance. One of the first responses I hear is "I hate that word hospice." Unfortunately, yes, even the word hospice makes people uncomfortable. In people's minds hospice = dying. So, if I'm in hospice care or my loved one is in hospice care then death is right around the corner.

While this is not entirely wrong, it is overly simplified. Yes, people die under hospice care. The problem is that people wait too long to receive services through hospice and so their death, or the death of a loved one, comes quickly. This is not the result of being under hospice care, it is the result of the natural dying process. The quick death causes people to be afraid of hospice because they are afraid of death.

On the Way...

Another response I hear, which is related to the first, is "It's too soon for hospice." The truth is that hospice can begin when a patient's physician gives a prognosis of six months or less if the disease follows the expected course. There is no need to wait until the person is close to death before seeking out hospice. Proactively enrolling in hospice early in the final phase of the disease process, ensures that the patient and their family can receive the benefits available to them.

Through a multidisciplinary approach, hospice provides a wide range of services to people of all ages. Medical doctors, nursing staff, social workers, spiritual counselors, dieticians, hospice aides, therapists and bereavement counselors work with patients and their families. This team facilitates a holistic approach to providing care. Under hospice, patients and their families are surrounded by professionals who work together to ensure that compassionate care is provided. With this care and support, patients have better quality of life for as long as they live, and some may even outlive their expected prognosis.

More than anything else, hospice is a philosophy of care. It's not a place, it's not a diagnosis. Hospice recognizes that the dying process is a normal part of living. It focuses on pain control, comfort, and enhanced quality of life when cure is no longer possible. The goal of hospice is to provide compassionate and supportive care so that a person may live as fully and comfortably as possible in the last phase of life. Hospice seeks a peaceful and comfortable dying experience for individuals and their families.

The confusion and resistance around hospice stems from some common misconceptions. These misconceptions interfere with the willingness of individuals and their loved ones to receive hospice care. The following myths and truths about hospice care are provided by The Hospice Foundation of America.

Myth: Hospice is giving up

Truth: Hospice is medical care toward the goal of comfort and dignity for someone whose life is drawing to a close. It is, in fact, the "something more" for someone who has been told nothing more can be done for them.

Myth: Hospice is only for cancer patients

Truth: Not anymore. When hospice began in the U.S. in the mid-1970s, most hospice patients had cancer. Today, while many hospice patients have cancer, the majority have other life-limiting illnesses such as end-stage heart, lung or kidney disease, or Alzheimer's and other dementias.

Myth: Hospice is where you go to die

Truth: The majority of hospice patients receive care in whatever setting they call 'home'—which includes private residences, assisted living communities, hospitals and long-term-care facilities. In some instances, hospice is a 'place' for people whose pain cannot be adequately managed in their home setting.

Myth: Hospice means I'm going to die soon

Truth: Studies show exactly the opposite. Although hospice care neither hastens death nor prolongs life, patients with certain illnesses actually live somewhat longer with hospice care than those with the same illness who don't choose hospice care. And regardless of the illness, patient/family satisfaction with services received are consistently higher when hospice is involved.

Myth: You can't keep your own doctor if you enter a hospice program

Truth: Your family doctor or specialist is encouraged to remain engaged in your care. The Hospice Physician works closely with your doctor—who knows you better (medically) than anyone else—to determine the specific medical needs that will be addressed in your individual plan of care.

Myth: It is the doctor's responsibility to bring up hospice

Truth: While it is the physician's responsibility to determine whether a patient meets the medical eligibility criteria to receive hospice services, it is appropriate for the patient (or caregiver) to initiate the discussion if they choose. Since hospices consistently hear from their patients/families that they wish they had gotten hospice care sooner, it is a good idea to let the physician know, at the time of diagnosis, that you are open to discussing hospice care at the appropriate time.

Myth: Once you choose hospice care there is no turning back

Truth: You are free to leave a hospice program at any time for any reason without penalty. You can re-enroll in a hospice program any time that you meet the medical eligibility criteria.

Myth: If you choose hospice care you won't get other medical care

Truth: While the hospice team will provide all aspects of care for the illness that qualifies you for hospice services, you are still free to seek treatment for unrelated illnesses or conditions. For example, if you are receiving hospice care for heart disease, you can still get treatment for a broken bone.

Myth: Hospice requires a DNR (Do Not Resuscitate) Order

Truth: The purpose and benefit of hospice care is to allow for a peaceful passing in a comfortable and familiar setting like home with loved ones near. While many people wish to have a DNR to avoid unnecessary medical intervention and hospitalization, you are not required to have a DNR to receive hospice care.

Myth: All hospices are the same

Truth: There are thousands of hospices in the United States. If they participate with Medicare, as most do, they are required to provide certain services to the patient and documentation to the government. In that respect, they are the same. However, hospices may be nonprofit or for-profit; they may be community-based or serve many communities, cities or states from a central location; they may be independent or part of another organization such as a hospital, health system or private company. The point is that all hospices (that participate with Medicare) meet the same basic requirements although there likely are differences from one provider to the next.[1]

---

1 Dispelling Hospice Myths, copyright Hospice Foundation of America, 2018. Used with permission. https://hospicefoundation.org/Hospice-Care/Dispelling-Hospice-Myths

On the Way...

If you or someone you love is facing a life-limiting medical condition, I encourage you to reach out to your doctor and a local hospice agency in your area. All it takes is a phone call to begin learning more about how hospice may be able to support you and care for your loved one as that person moves closer to the end of their life.

PART ONE

The Short Stories

CHAPTER 1
On the Way

Let me tell you about my Mom. Her name was Mary Hazel Odette Smith. Friends called her Hazel. Everyone agrees that she was always on her way somewhere. Born on December 8, 1942, mom grew up in Raleigh, North Carolina. She met my dad, Gary Douglas Smith, while they were students in high school.

Mom became pregnant with me when she was 15 years old. Her parents were mortified so they sent her away to live with relatives. This did not disrupt the love that was shared between my mom and dad and so they were married in June of 1959. I was born in November of that year.

Daddy enlisted in the U.S. Army right out of high school so that he could provide for mom and me. Being an Army family kept us on the move to lots of different places, including: Oklahoma, Germany, Kentucky, Florida, Washington, D.C., Panama, Oklahoma for a second time, and then Ohio.

For the most part, Mom thrived as an Army wife. The most challenging years were the ones when Daddy was deployed to the demilitarized zone in Korea and his time in the Vietnam War. Mom enjoyed the variety of places she got to live, some more than others, and made lots of friends along the way.

I think our favorite place to live was in Panama. At least it was for me. We were stationed in the Canal Zone from 1970-1974. It was an exotic place, full of adventures and wildlife. We enjoyed exploring the jungle and searching for old treasures, riding the rickety train between the Atlantic and Pacific sides of the isthmus, watching ships pass through the canal, and shopping in the cities of Colon and Panama City.

We left Panama during my 10th grade year of high school. We were privileged to be in one of the last military family caravans that were allowed to drive from Panama, through Central America and into the United States. Three weeks in a Ford Pinto. That's a whole story in itself!

I married my husband Bob in 1979 while we were students in college. We graduated in 1981 and had two daughters. My sister, Jennifer "Jenny" Jennings, was born in 1966 while we were living at Fort Knox, Kentucky. Seven years younger than me, we seemed to both grow up as only children: independent, confident, and strong-willed. Jenny married her high school sweetheart and they had three daughters.

While stationed in Cincinnati, Daddy had a massive heart attack in the summer of 1982. With significant damage to his heart and an aortic aneurysm, there wasn't much that doctors could do. He was sent home from the hospital and told to avoid physical exertion and take it easy. Not long after that, he was medically discharged from the Army. They put their house on the market and started the process of moving to Raleigh. Sadly, the aneurysm ruptured before they could move, and daddy died in March of 1983. He was just 42 years old.

Mom and Jenny moved to Raleigh not long after dad died. At first, they lived with Bob and me. This was a stressful solution for everyone. Mom was grieving the death of her husband. Jenny was grieving the death of her father and was angry because she had to move before her senior year of high school. I was grieving the death of my dad, had a 17-month old daughter and was pregnant with my second child. Bob was caught in the middle of all the chaos.

On the Way...

Mom provided a lot of support to us after I was put on bedrest due to complications with my second pregnancy. After our daughter was born in May, we encouraged mom to find a house of her own, a place where she and Jenny could live and begin settling into their new reality. Mom found a lovely home in North Raleigh and Jenny enrolled in high school.

Grief hit mom hard. She struggled with organizing her life after daddy's death. She hated being at home and did everything she could to avoid being alone. She was not always on her best behavior. She argued with people in restaurants and stores. She spent a lot of time in bars which got her in trouble. She drove too fast and made some bad decisions which made life hard for her, Jenny, and my family.

Eventually, she started participating in healthy activities. She got involved in social events, joined several women's groups, and became active in a local Lutheran congregation.

After about a year, she decided to go back to work. She worked as an insurance agent, a food broker, and a teacher's assistant. She volunteered with organizations that care for the homeless, the differently-abled, and those who are food insecure.

Her favorite things to do were eating out, shopping, going to the movies, playing cards, reading, hanging out with her friends, and spending time with her granddaughters and their parents.

She loved to go places: a road trip to the mountains, an excursion to a nearby outlet mall; and day trips to just about anywhere. Her favorite place to be was the beach.

When she was financially able, Mom purchased a single-wide mobile home at Emerald Isle, on the coast of North Carolina. It was a perfect size for her, and she spent a lot of time there. This truly was her happy place!

She enjoyed hosting others at her beach house. It was especially fun when my family and my sister's family came to visit on the same weekends. Jenny and her husband took one of the bedrooms, Bob and I took the other. Mom would sleep on the couch and all five of her granddaughters slept on pallets on the floor in the living room. No doubt we were crowded, but thankfully we enjoyed each other's company and many wonderful memories were made in that beach house.

Mom enjoyed having personalized license plates. She got a #1GRAMMY plate to let everyone else know

On the Way...

that being a "Grammy" was the most important aspect of her life. Later, she got an ONTHEWAY plate because she wanted the world to know that her favorite activity was being on the way. It didn't really matter where she was going, as long as she was on the way.

In the spring of 2008, Mom started struggling with her health. Now, she was on the way to frequent doctor appointments. Eventually, her doctors discovered that she needed surgery to remove part of her upper intestines because of a nonmalignant mass.

Recovering from this surgery was harder than anyone anticipated. Mom was miserable. Her pain was out of control and nausea made it hard for her to keep anything down. She lost weight quickly. Dehydration and pain sent her to the emergency room many times.

In early June, the doctors determined that she was not healing well because she had lung cancer. The night that she received this news, many of us were at the hospital with her. The doctor who delivered the diagnosis was very matter-of-fact. He came into her room and, without paying attention to who was there, declared that she had advanced lung cancer.

Hearing the "C word" sent everyone into a tailspin, except Mom. She turned her concern to everyone else. First, she apologized for the insensitivity of the doctor and then she promised to "fight the disease with everything she had." This wasn't an unusual response from mom. From being rejected by her parents, to having a child at the age of 15, to living as an Army wife, and the premature death of her husband, Mom spent her life fighting against the odds.

They admitted Mom to the hospital so that additional tests could be run the next day. Unable to settle down, she was given some medication to help her sleep. We waited until she drifted off, then many of us returned to our houses. We spent the next several hours supporting each other and trying to wrap our heads and our hearts around this thing called lung cancer.

The next day, several of us went back to this hospital. It was clear that Mom had spent a lot of time thinking about her situation.

She said, "I quit smoking more than five years ago so that I wouldn't get lung cancer. This just isn't fair. If I'd known that I'd develop lung cancer anyway, I would have continued to smoke!"

Mom continued to remind us of this as her disease progressed. At some level it made us laugh but often

On the Way...

her sense of regret and outrage at what was happening caused sadness.

All we could do that day was agree that "Yes, cancer isn't fair." We admitted that we were just as confused and concerned as she was, and we promised that we would face this together. We didn't know at the time how short this journey would be, but we knew it would be unlike any journey we'd ever taken.

WIGIAT? God was present in the ups and downs of Mom's life. God's presence protected and guided her as a pregnant teenager, a young mother, an Army wife, a world traveler, a grieving widow, an enthusiastic grandmother, a generous friend, and a beloved child of God. God's presence comforted her at the news of her diagnosis and remained with her as she was on the way to an unfamiliar and often scary place known as cancer. God was present.

CHAPTER 2
The Brain

Hearing a diagnosis of cancer is very scary! It throws your life into turmoil as thoughts about treatments, prognosis, and schedules consume you. On top of that, telling your friends and family about what's happening means dealing with the tears and concerns of others even as you deal with your own pain and anxiety. Very quickly, cancer becomes all consuming!

Dealing with a medical crisis is mind-blowing. You experience a wide range of emotions, sometimes all at the same time. Trying to hold onto everything that is being explained to you is impossible while you are juggling emotions and the pressures of daily living.

One day mom, Bob, Jenny and I met at the doctor's office for one of her first appointments. Sitting in the

On the Way...

waiting room, the nurse called Mom back. All of us stood up to make our way to the exam room.

The nurse stopped us saying, "We only need to see Hazel."

Mom replied, "I need all of them to come with me."

The nurse responded, "There's really not enough space in the exam room for all of you."

Mom countered, "Take me to a bigger room."

Reluctantly, the nurse motioned for us to follow her. We stepped into an exam room and she told mom to sit down and wait for the doctor. Then she left the room.

A while later, she returned with some paperwork and told Mom, "For your family to hear information about her health, you need to sign these release forms."

Mom immediately took the pen that was offered and signed the forms.

From that point on, Mom identified us as "The Brain."

Thankfully, Mom recognized that she was not functioning at her best cognitively and emotionally. She wanted our support, our attendance at her appointments, and our participation in meetings with the doctors and nurses who managed her care.

Often at appointments she said, "I need to wait for "my Brain" to arrive before we go any further."

Bob provided the "get it done" perspective. If something needed to happen like a trip to the grocery store or hardware store, he was on it. If some repair was needed at the house, he was there with his tool box. He researched everything and helped the rest of us understand the medical jargon. Bob did whatever needed to be done to support Jenny and me and to help Mom through this process.

Jenny provided the "heart" perspective. She was keenly aware of the broken-hearted pain that everyone else was feeling, especially the grandchildren. Mom had five granddaughters: my daughters Amanda and Becky, and Jenny's daughters Jessie, Abi, and Maggie. Jenny wanted Mom to have as much interaction as she could with each of the granddaughters and her friends and other family members. She encouraged Mom to be fully engaged with the people in her life for as long as she possibly could.

On the Way...

This tender-hearted care was exactly what Mom needed.

I provided the "realistic" perspective. I tried to be as objective as I could be as Mom moved from diagnosis through the first round of treatment. My focus was on providing a safe place for her to talk honestly about what she was feeling and what she wanted to do. I reminded her that this was her life, that she was in charge of it. She felt comfortable talking with me about matters of faith, dying, and death. Because I've accompanied many parishioners in the journey of diagnosis and treatment, very little about what she said surprised me. This made it possible for me to stay present in the here and now of whatever was happening each day.

Together as "The Brain" we provided perspective, clarity, and the assurance that Mom was not on this journey alone. We promised that the three of us would be there with her every step of the way. We were all working full-time jobs so making it to every appointment was often challenging. On those days when one part of "The Brain" was absent, Mom would wisely say; "I'm missing part of my brain so bear with me."

We discovered that each of us dealt with what was happening differently and that events would trigger a wide array of emotions. So, when one of us got tired, frustrated, or simply needed a break, another part of "The Brain" was there to step in. And when it got really hard, and tough conversations needed to happen or hard decisions needed to be made, we came together so that no one carried the load alone.

At first, we struggled with asking for and receiving help from others. We told ourselves that we were the only ones who could care for Mom. The truth was that none of us wanted to miss anything, so we made every effort to always be together with her. This was exhausting! Over time we realized that we could not sustain this path by ourselves.

We talked with Mom about who she felt comfortable having around her, helping her, when one of us was not able to be with her. Mom identified some of her friends and gave us permission to reach out to them.

Thankfully, they were each willing to do whatever they could to help. This was hard for them, too, since these wonderful friends have known Mom for such a long time. They knew her when she was a strong and determined woman. Seeing her in a more frail and vulnerable condition was unsettling. Yet, they showed up when we asked them to and they always did what they could.

These dear people were invaluable to us. They brought meals, ran errands, drove Mom to appointments, and sat with her whenever they were needed. Their presence made it possible for us to work, rest, and tend to our own affairs. This was such a gift to Mom, "The Brain," and the whole family.

There is power and comfort in knowing that others are walking this path with you. As we adjusted to what was happening, we became more comfortable leaning into their presence and allowing them to care for us and for Mom, who was their loved one too.

Together, we demonstrated the power that a close-knit support system provides. Because we approached the situation from different perspectives, we were able to care for Mom in ways that she needed while supporting each other. Walking alongside Mom and each other made this difficult time bearable, holy, and precious.

WIGIAT? God's presence supported us as we tried to make sense out of what was happening in and to Mom's body. God's presence drew us closer together as we dedicated ourselves to caring for Mom the best way that we could. God was present with her doctors and other health care providers. God was present with our employers at the time and all those around us who made space for us to care for Mom. God was present.

CHAPTER 3
The Hospice Decision

After consulting with an oncologist, Mom started the first of what was going to be several rounds of chemotherapy. This first round was really hard on her. She lost a lot of weight, much of her hair, and all of her stamina. She was constantly nauseous.

When the doctor talked with her about a second round of treatment, Mom was skeptical. The first round didn't do much to kill the cancer, so she didn't expect the second round to do much either. Still, while dreading the treatment and all of the side effects, she felt obligated to start another round.

One day, while driving her home from a treatment, she broached the subject of hospice. We talked about the criteria for entering hospice care, and the care and comfort they provide. Mom fell silent for a while and I let her rest in her thoughts.

On the Way . . .

Once we got home and I fixed our lunch, she brought up the subject again. This time she expressed concern about how others in the family would feel if she stopped treatment and entered into hospice care.

She said, "I don't want anyone to think of me as a quitter. I've never quit anything."

That was so true, Mom's life hadn't been easy. Yet she'd always persevered, pushing forward into whatever future was before her, always on the way to the next thing.

I replied, "Mom, you are the strongest woman I've ever known. Deciding to go under hospice care is a courageous decision, not a decision that a quitter makes."

She continued, "What if people are angry at me? I feel guilty making such a selfish decision."

My heart hurt for her as she struggled to sort out her feelings about what a decision to stop treatment meant.

I reminded her, "Mom, you are in charge of your medical care. This is your decision to make. We love you, and while some may not understand, we want you to be in less pain and at peace. We will support you."

Exhausted from the day and the difficult conversations we were having, she drifted off to sleep. This was really hard, and I was conflicted. I sincerely wanted her to make the best decision she could for herself, and I wanted her to be at peace with that decision.

Yet, I knew that the decision to stop treatment meant acknowledging that there was no cure. It meant admitting that death was inevitable, sooner rather than later. I also knew that continuing with treatment was only making her miserable and that she had no quality of life. This reality made me extremely sad.

The best way for me to cope was to approach this more objectively, to put my focus on Mom, rather than my own wants and needs.

While Mom was sleeping, I took time to do some research about different hospice groups in the Raleigh area. I compiled a list of questions for the doctor and hospice people. Even though I've traveled the hospice road before with some parishioners, it was different when it involved my Mom, me, and my family.

On the Way...

When she woke up, Mom seemed more at peace and announced that she'd made the decision. She said, "I want to stop treatment and enroll in hospice care immediately, before somebody tries to talk me out of it."

The first call we made was to the doctor's office. While I listened on another extension, Mom told the doctor that she was done with treatment. She explained that she wanted to enroll in hospice care and be kept as comfortable as possible until she died. It was a difficult call for her to make and for me to hear.

Doctors want to make people well. Oncologists want to conquer cancer. It's difficult for them to face the limitations of medical treatments. We weren't sure how the doctor would respond to Mom's decision. She was worried that she'd hurt his feelings by rejecting the treatment plan.

Thankfully, the doctor expressed relief about her decision. He indicated that even with the second round of treatment, her cancer was not curable. This was the first time that he so clearly stated the prognosis. He affirmed her decision to stop treatment and indicated that she was strong and courageous.

These were words that she needed to hear, words that gave her peace.

The doctor promised to do what he needed to do, including a referral to a local hospice agency. He asked her about setting up a "Do Not Resuscitate" order. This was frightening to her because it made what was happening very real. He explained that being under hospice care meant that you don't want life sustaining measures, including being resuscitated. Mom agreed that this was want she wanted so he signed the DNR order. I stressed to the doctor that mom wanted to enroll before the end of the day, in the hope that others would accept her decision once it was done.

Not long after the phone call to the doctor, a social worker from the hospice agency called to schedule a visit with Mom. The social worker provided information and answered our questions which made the intake visit go smoothly. Almost as soon as the social worker left, the nurse arrived. She collected a lot of medical information from us and explained the support services we would receive to keep Mom comfortable at home, things like regular visits by an aide and the use of medical equipment.

On the Way...

Mom explained that one of her biggest fears about dying was being in pain. This prompted the hospice nurse to assure her that the number one goal of hospice was to keep her comfortable and as free from pain as possible. This assurance put mom at ease.

The nurse ordered a hospital bed and a bedside commode so that Mom could stay in the family room around those who were caring for her. She compassionately reviewed everything, answered our questions, and then left.

Alone now, we had some time to process what happened so quickly that day. To my surprise, mom was upbeat and wanted to tell some of her friends about her decision. I think speaking to her friends helped Mom refine how she was going to talk about her decision with the family.

My sister, Jenny, came over to mom's after work. Mom was most anxious about talking with Jenny about her decision. She didn't want Jenny to be angry or disappointed with her. Thankfully, this conversation went well and after a few tears were shed by each of us, my sister came to understand the decision and Mom was relieved.

The decision to stop treatment and enter into hospice care is always hard, especially if the person is not incapacitated to the degree that death is imminent. Mom's cancer was pervasive and very advanced. It was clear that death would be the end of this story. But death wasn't going to come quickly.

The hospice nurse and social worker checked in every couple of days. This gave us the opportunity to keep life as normal as possible. Now that Mom wasn't undergoing treatment, she regained some energy and interest in life. When she was having a good day, we were able to go out to eat and do a little shopping. But when the day was more challenging, when she was feeling bad, she wanted to stay home and in bed. It was hard to be with her on those days because the reality of what was happening to her was very clear.

WIGIAT? God was present in my conversation with Mom. God's presence enabled me to be fully present with her as she processed what was happening to her and decided how she wanted to move forward. God's presence gave Mom rest and space in the midst of hard decisions. God was present in her medical team who received her decision and offered words of comfort. God comforted the family and friends when they heard the news that she had decided to stop treatment and enter into hospice care. God was present.

CHAPTER 4
"I Want to Die Right Now!"

The same day that Mom enrolled in hospice care, many of us gathered at her house for dinner. This gave her the opportunity to share her decision with everyone. Mom seemed peaceful and seemed to enjoy having everyone around.

It had been a long day. We noticed that she was falling asleep in her chair, so we said our good-nights. Everyone left for their own homes except Bob, who took the first shift and spent the night at her house.

Sometime in the night, Mom called out to Bob. He went to her bedroom where she was lying in her bed lamenting that hospice hadn't done what she thought they'd do. She was angry and disappointed.

On the Way . . .

She told Bob, "I'm ready to die. Kill me now or get the hospice nurse back here to do what she was supposed to do. Isn't that what hospice does?"

Bob explained to her, "I'm not going to kill you and hospice doesn't work that way. They don't cause you to die."

Mom said, "I feel like crap and I want this all to stop right now!"

Mom apparently thought that the purpose of hospice was to help the patient die whenever they're ready. And that was okay with her. In fact, that was what she expected from them. She was at peace with her situation and the fact that she had exercised her right to decide her future.

Bob reminded her that "the purpose of hospice is to keep you comfortable and as free from pain as possible while you die a natural death."

She'd heard that explanation earlier but was still having trouble wrapping her head around it all.

Bob continued, "Let's get some sleep and we can talk about this some more in the morning. Okay?"

Mom nodded her head, rolled over, and closed her eyes. It didn't take long before she was snoring. Still concerned about her, Bob decided to sleep in her room the rest of the night.

The next morning, I came to spend the day with Mom. The terms hospice and hospice care are confusing for everyone. The best way to gain clarity is to acknowledge our confusion and ask our questions.

Mom's hospice nurse stopped by to check on her and reviewed her medications. She spent as much time as she could answering our questions, providing guidance, and offering support. Her presence was a blessing!

She reminded us that the members of Mom's interdisciplinary team—herself, the social worker, heath care aide, chaplain, and doctor—were there for us. She reminded us that we were not walking this path alone and that we should seek out the help of our team whenever we needed them.

After she left, Mom asked me, "How long will it take me to die?"

This is probably one of the most asked questions when someone receives a terminal prognosis. We long for answers even when there aren't any.

On the Way...

Information, even if it's painful, helps us make sense of what's happening. It's a way for us to gain some bit of control over an uncontrollable situation.

I replied, "No one knows the answer to that question, Mom. The dying process is different for each person, and everyone dies in their own way and at their own pace."

Thankfully, Mom accepted this answer and didn't push me any further. She trusted that we were being honest with her, not withholding information from her. This trust enabled her to set aside her disappointment about what she thought hospice would do for her and turn her attention to living out her last days in the best way possible.

Mom asked, "What should I do now?"

This was a great question which gave us the opportunity to talk about what was important to her. I mentioned that one of the greatest gifts she can give to all those who love her was to show us how to die well. She asked me to explain what I meant:

"First," I said, "show us how to face death as a person of faith by drawing on the faith that has sustained you throughout your life. Second, show us how to interact with the people you love by allowing others to care for you during this time. And third, show us how to walk the path of dying with honesty and integrity by letting us know how you're feeling and what you're thinking so that we can walk alongside you."

We talked about the blessings of having more time with family and friends. Sitting together with a pad of paper, we made a list of everyone she wanted to see. We developed a strategy for reaching out to those people in hopes that she could speak with them before she died.

Then we made a list of things she wanted to do. This list included one more trip to the beach, movies she wanted to see, and restaurants she wanted to visit one more time. I stressed that this was a holy time, a time to enjoy the life that she had left doing whatever she wanted to do for as long as she could.

Mom said, "So, everything's going to revolve around me now?"

"Yes, Mom," I added, "This is your time and it's all about you."

"It's about time!" Mom replied with a big smile across her face.

On the Way...

We agreed to evaluate each day in order to decide what to do. On the days that she felt up to it, we'd go out to eat, or shopping, or to the movies. We'd attend worship or visit with a friend. On the days when she didn't feel good, we'd just read, watch TV, or simply take a nap.

WIGIAT? God's presence provided comfort to Mom and Bob that night as they tried to make sense of the hospice decision. God's presence helped Bob respond to Mom with compassion and courage. God's presence enabled Mom to accept the limitations of hospice and embrace living out her last days in the best ways possible. God was present.

CHAPTER 5
Taking Care of Business

Soon after enrolling in hospice care, Mom decided that she needed to take care of her business affairs. The first thing she wanted to do was make arrangements with a funeral home. At her request, I called the funeral home who handled my dad's arrangements. She felt good about how they handled things with daddy and trusted them to treat her with dignity.

We made an appointment for a funeral director to come to the house. He brought a brochure and quickly began reviewing everything with us. As Mom looked over the price list, her eyes narrowed, and a frown formed across her face. She shook her head. Seeing her visibly upset, I asked the funeral director to leave. He was hesitant and seemed more intent on signing her up for a plan, a plan for over $10,000.

On the Way...

The longer he stayed, and the harder he tried to persuade Mom to pick a package, the more anxious she became. Eventually, I was able to convince him to leave and promised that we would be in touch after we reviewed everything and made some decisions.

This funeral director just didn't quit. He called nearly every day to see if we'd made a decision. I kept putting him off because Mom wasn't ready to continue the conversation.

Finally, she brought it up saying, "That man from the funeral home was a jerk. I'm dying and all he could think about was selling me a funeral package. I don't trust him and don't want to give them any of my money."

When the funeral director called that day, he told me that because it was the end of the month, he really needed us to purchase a plan so that he could meet his quota.

"Really?" I said, "my mother is dying, and this is all you can say? Don't call here again, we're done with you and your funeral home!"

Both of us were angry at how she'd been treated through all of this. We talked about some alternatives and I suggested the Cremation Society. We made an appointment to meet with someone at their facility. This was a completely different experience.

The funeral director was compassionate and kind. She took time to get to know mom, to hear her wishes. Then she showed us a plan that would meet Mom's desires and still be affordable. Mom was pleased with this interaction and satisfied with what was shared with her, so we made the arrangements.

Several days later, we drove to the cemetery. When dad died, Mom purchased two cemetery plots next to each other. Because she decided to be cremated, she needed to purchase a vault to hold the urn. While taking care of this, mom asked if she could be buried over my dad's casket, in the same grave. They looked at her with compassion and explained that this question was asked quite a bit. Unfortunately, they told her that this was not allowed, that graves could only hold one person. She was clearly disappointed but assured us that she understood.

Her will was the next thing mom wanted to review. She prepared her will after Daddy died so the basics were in place. She called her lawyer who willingly came to the house to review everything with her. Mom made sure that Jenny and I were co-executors of her estate. She also named us as her medical and

On the Way...

fiduciary powers of attorney. All of this would make it less complicated for us to care for her and settle her affairs.

Plans for the memorial service was the next thing that she wanted to handle. Mom was a member and active participant in the ministries of Good Shepherd Lutheran Church for many years. She knew that this was where we will celebrate her life. We invited Pastor David Sloop to come over to Mom's house so that she could talk through the service with him. His compassionate presence was very calming to Mom. He encouraged her to pick all of her favorite hymns and scripture readings, which made Mom really happy.

After Pastor Sloop left, we got a pad of paper and began making a list of her favorite songs and hymns. With her well-worn Bible in hand, she selected the scripture readings for the service. After a while, we set this aside with the intention of picking it back up again whenever she wanted to add something to the list.

Mom was not the best housekeeper. There were piles of clothes, papers, and random things all over her house. She was reluctant to throw anything away, so collectables and antiques were everywhere. Shopping for bargains was one of her favorite things to do. She was in the habit of keeping shopping bags and items she'd purchased in one of her extra bedrooms until she needed them. With all this stuff strewn about, Mom's house was cluttered and unsafe, especially for someone who was unsteady on her feet.

The state of Mom's house had paralyzed her for a long time. Even though the whole situation made her feel uncomfortable and anxious, she had been unable to do anything about it. Her sensitivity about this caused her to keep people from coming to her house. She was afraid that they would be critical of her or think less of her.

Amanda, Jenny, and I tried to sort through the piles, throw out the trash, and clean things up while we were visiting with her. Mom had been resistant to help with her housecleaning in the past, so we did this while she was sleeping. One day, while Mom was resting in the living room, we headed to her bedroom to bag up some clothes that she no longer wore.

I'm not really sure why we decided to do this at this particular time. People who came to visit Mom would never see her bedroom. She was living in the family room at the time, so the state of her bedroom didn't really matter.

On the Way...

Maybe it was because we just needed something to do. There was so much we couldn't do, so much that was outside of our control. But we could clean her bedroom. We could bag clothes and donate them to others. We decided that this would be a great way to honor Mom. All the good intentions aside, it was great fun being sneaky while she was sleeping in another room.

One day, while "The Brain" was at work, Mom decided to run a couple of errands. It didn't occur to her, or to us, that it might not be safe for her to drive. She got herself ready and headed out. Sometime later, Mom called Jenny. She was sobbing and having trouble telling Jenny where she was.

Having grown up in Raleigh and returning to live here full time in 1983, Mom knew Raleigh like the back of her hand. She knew every short cut there was to get from one place to another. On top of that, she was a creature of habit, always going to the same grocery store, the same pharmacy, the same gas station, and the same restaurants. The reality that she was so confused about where she was and how to get home was sad and alarming.

All she could say on the phone was, "Come get me, come get me now."

Jenny kept her on the phone for a while, trying to settle her down enough so that she could describe her surroundings. Eventually, Mom was able to identify some landmarks which helped Jenny find her.

When Jenny arrived, Mom was sitting in her car at a gas station. Her head was in her hands and she was crying. Jenny opened the driver's side door and squatted down near her. She rubbed her back and comforted her with words of assurance, telling her that she was safe.

With tears still streaming down her cheeks, Mom handed Jenny her keys. She said, "Take my keys, it's not safe for me to drive anymore."

Jenny replied, "Oh Mom, this must be so scary! Let me drive you home."

Mom nodded her head in agreement and Jenny helped her move into the passenger's seat and they headed home. Jenny put the keys back in their usual place.

Getting lost and afraid upset Mom a lot. Her decision to surrender her car keys was a reality check for everyone and a brave action for Mom.

On the Way...

Much of what happens after a person enters into hospice care is related to surrender. Mom surrendered her privacy by allowing people to care for her. She surrendered the solitude of her home to accommodate those who were going in and coming out every day. She surrendered control over her schedule, her surroundings, and her belongings.

We tried our best to help Mom cope with those losses. We did that by making sure that she had opportunities to make decisions about things that mattered to her: what she wore, what she ate, what she wanted to do, who she wanted to see, and when she wanted company.

Taking care of business is a necessary part of getting a person's affairs in order. From financial and medical decisions to cremation arrangements and funeral planning, there are many preparations to make. Add to that, giving up car keys and letting others handle housecleaning. All of this makes things complicated. Emotions are raw. Stress abounds. Taking time to talk to each other and being sure to include the one who is dying are ways to cope with these challenging tasks.

I'm so thankful that, except for cleaning the bedroom, Mom initiated these conversations and facilitated the completion of these tasks. Because of her attention to these important things, handling everything after her death was less cumbersome and complicated. This was such a gift to the rest of us.

WIGIAT? God's presence helped Mom and the rest of us handle the financial and business affairs that needed to get done while she was still able. God's presence gave Mom the courage and strength to face obstacles and make wise decisions. God's presence comforted us as we faced the reality of her disease. God was present.

EXCURSUS 1

Mom's Generosity Affects Everyone

Generosity was one of Mom's greatest strengths. It was demonstrated in a variety of ways throughout her life.

One time, she sold one of our cars out from under us.

My uncle, Mom's youngest brother, had a teenage daughter who needed a car. Apparently at a family gathering, Mom and her brother were speaking about cars. Unbeknownst to us, she told him that we owned a five-year-old car which we'd just paid off and that she was sure we'd be happy to sell it to him for $5,000.

Next thing we knew, Mom called Bob into the room to tell him that she'd just sold our car for us. She said this right in front of my uncle which made it difficult

On the Way...

to challenge what she'd done. Mom genuinely thought she was doing us a favor and was proud of herself for brokering this "deal."

The reality was that we weren't planning to sell the car. We'd hoped to have a few more years without a car payment. But that's not how Mom works. In her mind, the car was paid off, so it was time to sell it and get a new one. Mom didn't give us an opportunity to object. Before we knew it, my uncle was handing us a check for $5000 and we were making arrangements to transfer the title. Mom was pleased with how she'd been able to help her brother and his family, and after a while, so were we.

Another time, Mom gave away one of her favorite quilts.

Mom loved to attend overnight church retreats. One winter, while at the camp, one of the other retreatants admired one of Mom's quilts. She spoke about how beautiful it was all weekend long. On the last day of the retreat, she mentioned again how much she liked it. Without hesitation Mom said, "Here, I'd like for you to have this." The woman quickly took hold of the quilt and expressed her appreciation. The next day, Mom voiced her own surprise at how easily she'd given away her quilt, saying, "I guess she needed it more than I did. But I really didn't expect her to take it!"

And yet another time, Mom became my secret shopper.

Bob is not a shopper. Shopping for my birthday and Christmas gifts was always a challenge. The couple of times he did it on his own did not go well. So, he worked out an arrangement with Mom. He gave Mom an allowance to spend and asked her to purchase what she thought I'd like. After shopping, she'd give him the bags of items so that he could wrap them. For many years, the two of them kept this a secret from me. This created a unique bond between them and always worked out well for me.

Mom's generosity overflowed into every aspect of her life. She was generous with her time, financial resources, and her possessions. More than all that, she was generous with her affection and love towards everyone. From her willingness to stop whatever she was doing to care for someone else, to oodles of gifts and surprise stops for ice cream, Mom's generosity was one of her greatest strengths.

CHAPTER 6
Surrounded by Love

There were many people supporting Mom and us in this journey. Each person was helping in ways that best used their skills and fit within their comfort zone and time parameters. We are forever grateful for the help and encouragement that they provided.

As soon as word of Mom's illness and her decision to go into hospice care was made public, she was flooded with greeting cards. She enjoyed opening them and reading the messages inside. When she could no longer do that herself, one of us would open them for her and read them to her. Each one brought a smile to her face as the loving words of others touched her deeply.

The cards were pouring in from every area of her life. At first the cards were collected in stacks for her to read. One night, while she was sleeping, Jenny and I

On the Way...

decided to hang the cards on the walls surrounding the room. We wallpapered all of one wall and then another. We spaced the cards out so that they didn't overlap each other. This made it possible to read the full message on the cover and inside the card

When Mom woke up to the sight of them, "hugging her," as she put it, she was filled with emotion. Those cards were a tangible sign of the love that others had for Mom and her family. That visible sign of her community filled her with peace and joy. As cards continued to arrive, she was eager for us to get them up on the wall as quickly as possible.

Jenny's daughters were members of the youth choir at their church. Mom enjoyed hearing the choir sing and frequently attended their concerts. One Sunday afternoon, 20 members of the choir and their parents surprised us with our very own concert. Spread out throughout the house, they sang some of mom's favorite songs. This brought so much joy to Mom and to the rest of us who were blessed by their visit.

On a Saturday afternoon several weeks later, we received a call from someone in a church Cristo community asking if it was a good day for some of them to stop by her house. After checking with Mom, we invited them over. Little did we know that this would be a group of more than 40 people. They squeezed into the house and overflowed into the front yard. Music is important in this community, so just as the youth had done, they serenaded us with beautiful and uplifting songs.

Several individuals set aside time to visit with Mom on a regular basis. Doug brought his dulcimer and sang to her. Peggy brought lotions to use as she massaged Mom's feet and legs, whispering prayers and words of encouragement. Laura came by to help us manage some details, locate missing items, and run errands. Robin was comfortable hanging out with Mom. Her presence always made Mom smile. CJ checked in on us nearly every day. She was willing to be called in the middle of the night if we needed help in any way.

Each one of these groups and individuals, and so many others, revealed God's love to Mom and to us in real and tangible ways. They showed up because they felt called to be there; because they loved Mom and they loved us.

Being care givers is isolating and lonely. You risk becoming so focused on the person you're caring for and the task at hand, that you easily lose sight of other relationships and responsibilities in your life. The presence and support of the individuals and wider communities helped us persevere in the task of caring for Mom. They reminded us that we were connected to a community that was bigger than ourselves. Their presence showed us that we were important to others and were not traveling this road alone. This was such a comfort and blessing to all of us.

WIGIAT? God's presence was evident in the loving cards and caring messages that people showered upon Mom and all of us. God's presence surrounded us with beautiful voices as people showed up to serenade us. God was present in the friends and family who visited and supported us throughout this journey. God was present.

CHAPTER 7
Nursing 101

Making the commitment to care for Mom at home was a huge responsibility. At first, the task seemed easy. Sitting and talking with her each day, watching TV, preparing meals, and helping her bathe, were all things we could do.

It didn't take long for us to realize, though, that this was going to be more complicated than we imagined.

Mom's lack of balance and the weakness in her legs made her a high risk for falling. The nurse encouraged her to use a walker when she moved about the house. Mom hated using that walker because it "slows me down." Early on, she'd "forget" to use it and then stumble into or over something. Sometimes she was able to catch herself on something but there were times when she actually did fall. We reminded her to be careful and asked her to let us help, but she was a

On the Way...

hard-headed woman. Eventually, she realized that avoiding a fall was essential to being able to stay at home.

Being alone in the house at night made Mom uneasy, so she asked that one of us spend the night with her. "The Brain" worked out a schedule so that we could make this happen. Thankfully, we had a couple of friends who were willing to spend the night too when one of us wasn't able to be there.

At first, we slept on the couch while she slept in her bed in the bedroom. This worked for a while. Eventually, her needs increased so we asked the hospice nurse to order a bed for her to use in the family room. This enabled us to be in close proximity to each other so that we could respond quickly to her needs.

Several medical situations tested the limits of our basic first aid and CPR training.

Mom received fluids through an IV to help deal with the dehydration she faced. She needed several bags each day, so the nurse gave us two options: admit Mom to the hospital or learn how to change the bags at home. Mom was fearful of going to the hospital because she was afraid that she'd never return home. Because staying in her home was important to Mom, we agreed to do what we needed to do to keep her there. This meant learning to change the bags ourselves.

The nurse explained the protocol while we frantically wrote down the step-by-step instructions. Dealing with the medical side of things made us uncomfortable. We were afraid of doing something that would cause Mom more pain or result in her death.

The nurse explained the importance of hand washing so that we wouldn't expose Mom to any germs. Then she showed us how to prime the IV tubing before placing the next bag to avoid causing an air embolism. Making sure that the fluid was flowing at the appropriate rate meant that she was getting the level of fluids at the pace she needed. All of this heightened my fear and made me more diligent as I carried out the tasks at hand.

Mom knew the procedures too, so she made sure that we followed every step. If we got something out of order, she was very quick to correct us saying, "Pay attention! This is my life you're dealing with!"

We'd take a deep breath, make eye contact with her, and then a little smile would emerge across her face. She'd say, "It's okay, I know you've got this."

On the Way...

Whew! Crisis averted. After handling this process successfully, a couple of times, everybody got more comfortable, the tension lessened, and the fear subsided.

Little did we know that learning to change IV bags would come in handy when dealing with the next complication.

Mom developed a fever and was feeling miserable. She was complaining of pain under her left armpit. We looked and noticed a rash developing. At the next nurse's visit, she looked at the rash and told us that she was concerned that it could be MRSA, a serious and resistant staph infection.

The nurse wanted Mom to go to the emergency room to be checked by a doctor. Mom wasn't happy with the idea of going to the ER. The nurse explained the importance of an accurate diagnosis and treatment plan so that the infection didn't spread. Eventually, the nurse was able to persuade Mom to go, so she called the hospital to alert them that we were on our way.

We arrived at the hospital and discovered that they were waiting for us. They worked quickly to get Mom into a treatment room. The ER was crowded, and many were waiting to be seen, so walking past them was uncomfortable. We were thankful, though, for the ER staff who helped Mom avoid exposure to whatever brought others to the ER.

The doctor and nurses worked quickly to run tests and determined that it was indeed MRSA. Once again, we were given the options: admit Mom to the hospital for treatment or take her home and do the treatment there. Knowing how she felt about being in the hospital, we decided to take her back home.

Because we'd learned how to manage IV's earlier, we felt pretty good about handling this part of her treatment. The big difference was that this time the IV contained antibiotics that would be going directly into her heart through the port of her PICC line.

So much about this gave us anxiety. The risk of introducing an air embolism into her PICC line and the possibility of introducing more germs into her already fragile immune system meant that we had to be even more careful than before.

Dealing with ointment and dressing changes at the site of the MRSA infection put us at risk. The nurse stressed that we needed to do everything we could to protect ourselves from the infection. Lots of handwashing, wearing gloves, and careful attention to what we were doing and where our hands were at all times was the only way to address this risk.

Caring for mom at home was harder than we thought it would be for several reasons. First, it required more than basic first aid and CPR training. Dealing with IV fluids and antibiotics, changing dressings, and managing medications made us feel like we had completed a Nursing 101 class!

Second, we learned that teamwork and collaboration were essential to providing in home medical care. There is so much that needs to be done and expectations are extremely high because you're dealing with the life of your loved one.

Yes, even though your loved one is dying, how you provide care helps them continue to live as comfortably as possible. There isn't much room for error when you are providing medical care, so having others around who can double check your work, help problem solve, and encourage you along the way is a blessing.

Fear and anxiety, love and commitment, are normal reactions to being on the way with a loved one in hospice care. You make the decision to care for someone at home because you love them deeply and you want to honor their desire to die at home.

Nothing about this is easy but all of this is doable because of your efforts, the collaboration of others, and the support of a skilled and attentive hospice team.

WIGIAT? God's presence enabled us to care for Mom in ways that stretched beyond our comfort zones. God was present in caring nurses and aides and in the medical staff at the hospital. God's presence gave us the courage and strength we needed to be fully committed and intentional about caring for Mom. God's presence steadied our hands and settled our thoughts so that we could follow the treatment plans that were in place. God was present.

CHAPTER 8
Managing Medications

Mom was plagued by intense nausea. This made it hard for her to keep anything down, including food, drinks, and medications. Mom's way of dealing with this was to avoid eating or drinking anything. The hospice nurse tried a variety of medications to eliminate her nausea but because it was difficult to take the pills, Mom wasn't getting any relief.

We tried a variety of strategies to find an easier way for her to take her meds—crushing and mixing them in applesauce and dissolving them in water for her to sip. Nothing was working. She got to the point where just looking at her pills caused her to gag.

Bob searched the internet to research creative ways to treat nausea and stumbled upon medications for motion sickness. These come in patches that you

On the Way...

wear behind the ear. It was worth a try, so he headed to the pharmacy to pick up a pack.

Thankfully, they made a difference and Mom started to feel better. When we reported this to the nurse, she helped us get a higher therapeutic dose through the hospice pharmacy.

Now that the nausea was managed, we set out to make sure that Mom took her medications when she was supposed to. She was on eight medications for things like diabetes, high blood pressure, high cholesterol, thyroid replacement, depression, GERD, and pain control. It was so complicated! Some she took in the morning, some at lunch time, and some before bed. Because she hadn't been taking them regularly and was so fuzzy headed, she was having trouble remembering what to take and when to take it.

"The Brain" decided to tackle this problem. We gathered all of the medication bottles, read the labels, and tried to make sense of it all.

The three of us sat around a small table in her kitchen with all of the pill bottles in front of us. Bob got a piece of paper and created a grid with several columns and rows. We noted the name of the medication, when it needed to be taken, the color, and the shape of the pill.

At first the list of medications was random, in the order that we picked up the pill bottles. After using this list for a day or two, we decided that this configuration wasn't helpful, so we threw away that chart and made a new one.

This time we alphabetized the names of the pills and noted all of the same information. But this process was still cumbersome and confusing. After a day or two, we decided to make a new chart.

"How do we want this chart to help us?" I asked.

Jenny said, "Well, I think it would work best if the pills are grouped according to when they need to be taken."

We looked at each other, and Bob said, "That certainly makes sense! Why haven't we thought of that before?"

We broke into laughter—laughing about our compulsion to get this just right, laughing about the amount of time we've spent moving pill bottles around. Just laughing!

On the Way...

The design of the third chart worked well. All of the pills she needed to take in the morning were in one section, the afternoon pills in another, and a third section listed the pills she needed to take before she went to bed.

With a working chart in hand, we moved on to make a checklist so that we could track the pills she took. This would help us make sure that she didn't duplicate any pills. We also started a small notebook so that we could leave notes for each other. All of this helped us take control of an otherwise uncontrollable situation, but drove Mom crazy.

At first, she laughed at us for spending so much time paying attention to her medications. But later she expressed a lot of frustration at us exclaiming, "Let me worry about my meds!"

We'd inadvertently set up a power struggle between us and Mom. We wanted her to take her medications and she wasn't interested in taking them. We'd become preoccupied with dispensing these pills which caused frustration for everyone.

The truth was that we needed this task so that we could feel like we were doing something to help. At the same time, though, Mom was sad because she realized that she was losing control over her life and her body.

Unfortunately, we didn't recognize and understand her struggle. We missed how much she was hurting because of her situation. We were too focused on making sure that Mom took her medications that we lost sight of Mom as a person. Our attempt to help caused her nothing but frustration and anxiety.

We shared our frustrations about all this with the hospice nurse and she gave us a wonderful gift saying, "You know your mother is dying, right?

I replied, "Yes, we know that. But she needs to take her medications, right?"

Nurse: "Well, maybe not. Because she's dying, she really doesn't need some of these medications."

"Really?" I asked.

"Yes, really-" the nurse said, "It won't hurt her to miss her blood pressure and cholesterol medications."

I pushed back a little harder saying, "Are you sure?"

"At this point, it's the cancer that's killing your mom, not high blood pressure or high cholesterol," the nurse explained.

On the Way...

"That certainly put everything in perspective," I pondered out loud.

Mom was thrilled and relieved! Finally, she saw a way out of having to take those meds. She talked with the nurse about what she needed to take each day and what she could do without.

Then the nurse told us not to worry if she missed any of her medications. She explained, "Try to take them, and if you can't get them down one day, don't worry about it."

This was such a blessing. The nurse gave us permission to stop worrying about her medications. She set us free from the burden that was consuming us. This blessing was a huge gift for all of us.

Knowing what to focus on was a balancing act, it was an art. There were no easy answers. We allowed ourselves to get distracted and didn't take a step back to evaluate what we were doing.

We forgot that we were caring for a person, not managing a project. We lost sight of Mom as the reason for everything we did, every decision we made. Maintaining communication with her and others on the team would have helped us alleviate our anxiety and frustration and not caused any for Mom. Our over-focused attention on her medications diminished Mom's capacity to make her own decisions. We put ourselves in the role of medication monitors, which took away her sense of self, her dignity, her power. This realization was hard to swallow. Yet it helped to get us back on track.

WIGIAT? God showed up in our deep desire to care for mom. While we may not have shown it in the best way, we really were trying to help. God showed up in the gift of our hospice nurse who spoke words of truth. God showed up in the love of our mother who was, on one hand, totally frustrated with us and, on the other hand, totally forgiving of our misplaced priorities.

EXCURSUS 2

Mom's Reaction to a Surprise Birthday Party

Mom loved parties! She enjoyed everything about them: inviting guests, decorating, shopping for the supplies, and preparing food. When Mom's 50th birthday was on the horizon, Jenny and I decided to plan a surprise birthday party for her.

We sent invitations to all of her friends. Decided to use a black buzzard as the theme for the party. We got black balloons and black plates and napkins. My house was decorated with black streamers and other party decorations. Jenny's husband, David, made a black buzzard cake.

We worked out the arrangements with a couple of her friends to take her to one of her favorite restaurants for dinner before they brought her to our house for dessert. They enjoyed a nice meal and a couple of

On the Way...

glasses of wine with dinner. After they finished dinner, one of her friends told her that they were expected at our house for dessert. This was the first part of the surprise.

Everyone gathered inside and anxiously waited for mom to arrive. When she walked in the door, we yelled "Surprise!" and Mom seemed genuinely surprised to see everyone.

Mom greeted everyone who was there and enjoyed having conversations with her dear friends. There was a lot of laughter and fun, with loud conversations as these friends enjoyed this time with Mom.

A friend made a video collage with pictures of mom through the years. Photos of Mom with all of her favorite people, including daddy. As we watched this together that night, laughter and tears flowed freely.

The party lasted for several hours while everyone enjoyed the cake and snacks. Eventually, people started saying their goodbyes and thanked us for the opportunity to celebrate with Mom. We were thrilled that the party went so well.

That didn't last long. After everyone left, Mom expressed anger about the party. It turned out that she hated being surprised. She hated the buzzard image and all of the black decorations. We tried to explain that we were only trying to make her birthday fun—but she wouldn't hear us.

Instead she pouted about the party for weeks. We felt horrible. Eventually, she told us that the reason she was so upset about the party was that she hated getting older.

Mom seemed to fight aging at every turn by taking every opportunity to stay young. She enrolled in dance lessons, joined book clubs, learned new card games, played with her grandkids, completed sewing projects, got active in her faith community, took international and domestic trips, and participated in a wide variety of community service opportunities. This kept her active and made her young at heart and in spirit until the end of her life.

CHAPTER 9
Hazel's Team

It was a typical day at Mom's. Jenny and I were there with her. We were watching daytime TV and talking about whatever came to mind. Mom was relaxed and resting in her bed in the family room.

Somehow, she'd gotten herself into an uncomfortable position, slouched down and crooked. She complained and asked us to help her get more comfortable in the bed. We'd watched and helped the nurse adjust her position by using the sheet under her, so we figured this should be pretty easy.

Jenny got on one side of the bed and I got on the other side. We explained to Mom that we were going to count to three and then work together to move her up in the bed. She was eager to get more comfortable and we were eager to get her settled, so we counted to three and lifted.

On the Way...

But, instead of pulling her up at the same time, one of us pulled her up right as we said three and the other waited until after we said three. It was a minor issue but still resulted in Mom becoming even more crooked in the bed.

Jenny and I started laughing at what we'd done or failed to do. But Mom didn't think it was funny at all. We explained that we were laughing at ourselves for making such an easy task so complicated. She was still not amused and became very agitated. We tried to persuade her to let us try again but she refused.

Jenny said, "Mom, we've got this. We know what we did wrong, so we'll be sure to do it right the next time."

We took our positions by her bed and got ready to move her again, but Mom stopped us saying, "There won't be a next time. I'm even more uncomfortable now so get me out of this bed and into my wheelchair right now."

Trying to hold back laughter and seeing how angry she was, we helped her get in her chair.

After she got settled in her chair, she told us to sit down on the couch. Then she demanded that we call Robin, one of her friends, to come over.

I asked, "Why do you want Robin to come over? She's at work right now."

Mom said, "I just need Robin to come over. We won't talk until she gets here."

We looked at each with befuddled faces. I made the call to Robin and explained as best I could what was going on. She agreed to come over as soon as she could.

I told Mom that Robin was on the way. Every time Jenny and I tried to talk with each other or Mom, she shushed us. She demanded that we sit in silence until Robin arrived.

And that is exactly what we did as we watched the clock and waited.

After a while, the hospice nurse arrived. She found Jenny and me on the couch and Mom sitting in her wheelchair. She wondered what was going on. Mom told her that we were waiting for Robin to arrive so that we could work some things out.

The nurse tried to begin her visit, but Mom shushed her too. Mom told the nurse, "We need to wait for Robin to get here before we start anything." The

On the Way...

nurse looked at her watch and then sat down on the couch with us.

Jenny and I looked back and forth at mom, the nurse, and each other, fighting back laughter. We sat in silence, endless silence, watching the clock and waiting.

Finally, Robin arrived. Mom instructed her to join Jenny and me on the couch. The nurse sat nearby.

With much seriousness, Mom said, "You're all on Hazel's team. Everything you do is about being on Hazel's team. Hazel is not a sack of potatoes to toss around, and you need to stop fussing with each other."

Yes, she spoke of herself in the third person.

I responded, "Mom, I think you've misunderstood our laughter. We're not arguing with each other, we're just laughing at our inability to move you up in the bed. We thought it would be so easy, but it's not easy at all."

Mom replied, "Well, it's not funny. You're not acting like you're on Hazel's team right now. Whose team are you on?"

Jenny replied, "Mom, we're sorry we've upset you. We're on your team, we promise. We're trying to take care of you the best way that we know how."

Mom continued to lecture us, "Remember, you're on Hazel's team and Hazel is the one who matters now. You're expected to play nicely with each other and take care of Hazel. Do you agree to do that?"

We agreed and apologized again, then sat in awkward silence for a few minutes.

After a while, Mom allowed the nurse to check her medical condition and then Mom asked to get back in bed. Thankfully, the nurse was able to show us how to move Mom up in the bed safely, easily, and comfortably. Once she was settled in the bed, Mom drifted off to sleep.

Exhausted from the stress of the afternoon, the nurse, Robin, my sister, and I went outside for some fresh air. As we recalled what just happened, all we could do was laugh and cry together at the absurdity of it all.

It was a therapeutic laugh for all of us. Laughter is good. It's helpful. Laugh when you need to laugh. Laugh when you want to laugh!

On the Way . . .

Jenny and I continued to talk about what happened earlier in the day, Mom's strong reaction, and what we should have done differently. We realized that we didn't include Mom in the conversation about how we were going to move her up in the bed. We didn't check to make sure that she was on board and didn't give her the opportunity to help us in the process. Had we done all that, she wouldn't have been surprised by our actions and maybe things would have gone better.

Figuring out all of this led us to change our approach to caregiving, instead of taking charge, we committed to giving Mom every opportunity to participate in, even direct as she was able, the care that she was receiving. The hope was that this would honor her, keep her comfortable, and make the journey more peaceful and lifegiving for everyone.

WIGIAT? God was present in the compassionate nurse who gave hours of her time to meet Mom's needs that afternoon. God was present in our dear friend Robin who stopped what she was doing to come over to Mom's house. God was present in Mom's courage to speak her mind and tell us what she needed, even if she went about it in an odd way. God was present in our laughter and in our tears as we tried to make sense of what happened that day. God was present in it all.

CHAPTER 10
Trip to the Beach

The beach was Mom's favorite place to be! She loved sitting on the beach and letting the water come up over her feet. She enjoyed walking along the beach and collecting seashells along the way. There was something about the beach that made her happy and relaxed.

There are so many memories associated with being at the beach with Mom, things like the many weekends all 10 of us crammed into her single wide mobile home, frequent trips to her favorite seafood restaurant, the children rinsing off in the pool in her back yard, the long walks to get to the beach weighed down like pack mules, and the joy of watching the children play in the sand and in the water.

When Mom enrolled in hospice care, we talked about the things she wanted to do while she was able. Going

On the Way ...

to the beach was the first thing she mentioned. Before we made any plans, we checked with the hospice team to make sure that it was safe for her to travel. They gave us the okay, so we got busy preparing for the trip.

We all knew that taking mom to the beach was a risk. A medical emergency far from her hospice team could develop. Problems with her IV might come up. The trip might exhaust her, causing a negative impact on her overall well-being. Mom knew the risk. We knew the risk. With the support of her hospice team, we decided to go for it.

It was near the end of September so finding a rental place wasn't hard. The hard part was figuring out what we needed to bring with us. Mom was on an IV to prevent dehydration, so we needed to bring all of those supplies. She needed her walker and bedside commode. She needed her portable oxygen tank and her medications. Plus, she needed clothes for a few days.

Mom had driven herself to the beach so many times that the trip should have been easy for her. Yet this time, the three-hour drive was hard. Sitting for so long made her very uncomfortable, so we needed to stop frequently to allow her to stretch her legs.

Midway through the drive, I reclined her seat so that she could lie down a bit.

She was exhausted when we arrived. Soon after getting her into the house she went right to bed. We took this time to settle in, rest, and prepare a meal. Mom woke up for a while. She ate some dinner and spent some time with us. The house was crowded and noisier then she was used to, so the commotion tired her out.

It was cool and windy the next day. Even though we were in a beachfront property, it was a long walk to the water. The cold air, wind, and distance made it clear that Mom wasn't going to make the walk down to the beach. So, we sat with her on the porch and looked at the ocean. She was relaxed and talkative.

Mom said, "This is wonderful! Thanks for getting me here."

"You're welcome, Mom," I replied, "I love it here, too."

Lamenting, Mom said, "I really wish I could put my toes in the sand."

Jenny replied sadly, "I know. We'd hope that you'd be able to do that. It's why we got a beachfront place."

On the Way...

We sat for a while just looking at the ocean and listening to the wind and waves.

After thinking through the options, one of the granddaughters decided to collect some sand in a baking pan. She brought the sand to mom. The sand was a little damp but that didn't stop Mom. She sat with her feet in the sand for quite a while, with a big smile on her face.

Mom said, "This is exactly what I wanted to do. Thank you for making it happen!" After a while, her feet got cold and she was tired, so we helped her go back inside for a nap.

We sat on the porch a while longer, feeling satisfied that we'd been able to get her to the beach. It was a bittersweet moment.

She slept quite a bit while we were at the beach and didn't feel up to going back outside. The rest of us took time to relax and enjoy the beach ourselves. We tried to make the best of the weekend.

After the trip, Mom continued to express deep appreciation for the time and effort it took to get her to the beach and back home safely. Even though we felt a deep sadness at the realization that this was Mom's last time to the beach, seeing the contentment on her face and hearing the joy in her voice made the effort worth it.

WIGIAT? God was present in each person who helped mom get to the beach. God was present in the crisp wind that blew through the air. God was present in the sound and power of the ocean, in every grain of cool sand that comforted mom that day. God was present.

CHAPTER 11
The Talking Stick

Mom felt like everything around her was in chaos. She was struggling with getting around the house. She required assistance to take care of her basic needs like dressing and bathing. She'd lost her privacy and her capacity to be independent. She was no longer in charge of her days and had to deal with lots of people in her house. All of this affected her mood and quality of life.

There was a lot of activity at Mom's house most days and this day was no different. Jen, the hospice nurse, the hospice aide, and I were at Mom's house at the same time. The nurse was checking on Mom's physical health while the home health aide was changing her bedding. Jenny and I were handling things in different rooms. Mom was sitting in her wheelchair as all of this was happening around her.

On the Way...

Everyone was talking and moving around. It was loud as we spoke to each other from different rooms, talking over each other. No one seemed to be listening. Finally, Mom couldn't stand it anymore.

She demanded, "Stop what you're doing right now, sit down, and be quiet!"

Surprised by the intensity of her words and the tone of her voice, we promptly did what she asked us to do.

She waited for us to comply. Her face was tense, her eyes were filled with tears, and her voice was weak.

She said, "You're driving me crazy. Stop talking. Stop ignoring me!"

"Mom, we're sorry." I replied, "We just got carried away." Mom interrupted me and told me to bring her a wooden spoon. "Okay, but what do you need that for?"

Mom said, "Just bring me the spoon." So, off I went to the kitchen to find a wooden spoon which I brought back to Mom.

Spoon in hand, Mom said, "Because everyone is talking at the same time, you'll now use this spoon as the Talking Stick."

The Talking Stick was a tool that Mom used while she was active in Girl Scouting. The Talking Stick works this way: the leader passes the stick to someone who wants to speak; they speak for as long as they want or need to; no one else speaks. Once they've said what they want to say, they pass the stick to someone else who then has the opportunity to speak. For a group of Brownie and Junior Girl Scouts, the Talking Stick is an essential way to manage conversation. It's apparently helpful with a group of grown women too, at least Mom thought so.

It was difficult not to laugh at what was happening. There was my Mom, very sick, sitting in her wheelchair, ordering four women to sit down and use a Talking Stick if we wanted to speak. The nurse and home health aide looked at Jenny and me for insight into what was happening. Before we could explain, Mom continued to exert her authority.

She looked at the nurse and said, "You're the nurse, so you get to go first. Here's the Talking Stick. What do you want to say?"

On the Way . . .

After the nurse spoke, Mom passed the stick to the hospice aide, and invited her to speak.

Then the stick was passed to Jenny and then to me.

Finally, mom held the Talking Stick. She took her turn and reminded us, "You are all on Hazel's team and on Hazel's team everybody listens to each other and waits to speak until they are holding the stick. So, stop talking over each other and wait your turn."

We apologized for upsetting her and agreed that we'd do better.

After a while, the nurse and the home health aide helped Mom get back in bed. They made her comfortable and it wasn't long before she drifted off to sleep. Jen and I walked with them outside for some fresh air to relieve the tension we'd experienced that afternoon.

Back inside Mom was sleeping peacefully. When she woke up, she was eager to talk. I asked her if she wanted to use the Talking Stick and she looked at me with confusion.

After explaining what happened earlier in the day, Mom expressed disbelief until we showed her the "stick." Sitting there in her bed, holding the spoon, she enjoyed a good laugh as we reminisced about her time as a Girl Scout leader and about how she had controlled four women with a wooden spoon.

While we could laugh about what happened, Jenny and I felt badly about upsetting Mom. Talking about the interactions that afternoon, we recognized that Mom gave us hints about her state of mind which we missed: she was quieter than usual, her head was slumped down, her facial expression was tense, and she was wringing her hands. Had we been paying attention to her, we would have noticed those behaviors and adjusted how we were interacting with each other. As her caregivers, we needed to intentionally pay attention to her so that we could help her cope in the stressful times.

WIGIAT? God was present in the members of the hospice team who responded lovingly to Mom's reaction that day. God was present in the memory of the "Talking Stick." God was present in our renewed commitment to more intentionally pay attention to Mom's needs. God was present in the loving interaction between Jenny and me as we tried to get through that day. God was present in a wooden spoon that allowed Mom to have some control over an uncontrollable day. God was present.

EXCURSUS 3

Mom Saved Me from Deadly Laundry

While stationed at Fort Davis in the Canal Zone of Panama, we lived in a townhouse at the end of a building with four units. Each unit had an attached utility room just outside the back door which housed a washer and dryer.

One day after school, Mom sent me to get the clothes out of the dryer. The dryer was cold, so I knew that the clothes had been in there for a while. I reached inside to pull the clothes out. To my surprise, the clothes in my arms were moving! Something cold and slimy rubbed against my arm and the head of a snake started to protrude.

I dropped the clothes onto the floor of the utility room. The snake slithered out and coiled up between me and the door.

On the Way . . .

Standing as still as I could, I thought through everything I knew about the kinds of snakes that live in Panama. The dark grey, broad, flattened, triangular head on this snake told me that this was a fer-de-lance, one of the most venomous snakes in the region.

The snake just laid there looking at me. There was no way for me to move past it. So, I just stood there, trying not to startle it. I called out to Mom in my normal voice, but she was inside the house and didn't hear me.

A shovel was in the corner near me. I picked it up slowly and used it to tap on the wall that connected the utility room to the house hoping that Mom would hear me. Of course, she didn't.

So, I just stood there as still as I could. I stared at that coiled up fer-de-lance praying that it wouldn't strike me. The snake was also being very still, watching me, and probably wondering what I was going to do.

At last, Mom came outside looking for me. Just before she entered the utility room, in as calm a voice as possible, I told her to stop. Seeing the concerned look on my face, Mom came to a complete stop and looked at me. She said, "What's going on?"

I pointed to the snake coiled up between us. With his head raised and mouth open, his fangs were easily visible. It was clear that he was ready to defend himself, ready to strike, if he felt threatened in any way.

The three of us kept looking at each other. Mom grabbed the broom propped in the corner near her. I held the shovel in my hands. Together we struck the snake. The snake moved toward me, trying to get away. I used the shovel to hit him again and then Mom hit him again with the broom until he eventually stopped moving.

We stood there looking at each other and the snake for what seemed like minutes, waiting for it to move again. Finally, we concluded that the snake was dead. I gathered up the laundry, now dirty from the snake and being on the floor, and I tossed it into the washer before heading inside.

The next time I went to get the laundry out of the dryer, I used a stick to poke the clothes. I'd wait a few seconds then poked them again. Each time I'd wait to see if a snake would crawl out. Once I was sure that there wasn't anything extra in the dryer, I'd reach in to get the clothes. I'm happy to report that I never discovered a snake in the dryer again.

CHAPTER 12
The Branch

Mom was sleeping a lot and when she was awake, she was very quiet. Conversations seemed to take a lot out of her.

Some people, when facing the end of their physical life, may turn to spiritual things, others may not. We tried to let Mom set the pace of each day. She determined what we talked about. If she wanted to talk about faith, life, and death one day, that's what we talked about. If she wanted to be silent one day, we honored that. If she wanted to tell us stories of her life, we listened carefully. If she wanted to talk about final things, we paid attention to that.

Dying was a spiritual journey for Mom. She often wanted to talk about matters of faith. Having those conversations was important to her and therefore important to us. We worked hard to create a space

On the Way...

where she felt safe to ponder out loud, ask her questions, and put words to her doubts and anxieties.

One day, she started a conversation with me about dying and death.

"What will it be like? she asked.

"I don't really know, Mom, medically," I explained, "your breathing and heart rate will slow down until you finally drift off into sleep, the sleep that is death."

She said, "I hope it's not painful."

Offering assurance, I promised, "We'll do everything we can to keep you comfortable and as free from pain as possible."

She was quiet for a while and then she said, "Tell me that it's all true."

"That what's true?" I asked.

She clarified, "That everything I've read and heard about God and heaven are true."

Hearing the profound sadness and genuine concern in her voice caused my heart to break. I knew that mom wasn't losing her faith. She wasn't giving up on God.

Instead she was longing to be reminded of the powerful promises of God.

I took her hand into mine and we prayed together. Then I picked a couple of scriptures to read and we talked about the promises that God made to us and for us.

I reminded her that "Facing death himself, Job knew that he would see God," and I assured her, "You too, will see God, when you gather at the feast that has no end."

She thought about this for a minute and then lamented the struggle that Job faced in his life. We talked about that a little bit and then recalled how God restored him in the end. Then we reviewed the many ways that God restored Mom throughout her own life and I offered the assurance that God would restore her one more time.

I reminded Mom of the words of Jesus from John 14, "Mom, Jesus has prepared a place for you in God's house. A place where there is no more pain, no more illness, no more crying. And sometime soon, Jesus promises to take you to himself. This is God's gift to and for you."

On the Way...

Mom pondered out loud about God's house. It made her chuckle as she wondered what the rooms looked like and if she'd have a roommate. We concluded that Daddy was already there waiting for her.

The last passage I shared was from Romans 14:7-8, but rather than read the passage to her, I summarized it like this, "Mom, remember that God has been with you throughout your life, carried you through some really tough times. You belonged to God then just as you belong to God now. And when you die, you will still belong to God. Not even death separates you from God."

We sat in silence for a few minutes. Mom was deep in thought.

After a while she said, "These are beautiful passages. They sound very promising. I just hope that its true for me."

"Mom." I said. "Jesus is holding you tightly in his love right now."

She smiled, closed her eyes, and said, "I'm tired. I'd like to sleep."

I sat with her for a while, just looking at her as she slept. Finally, I wandered outside.

It was a beautiful November day. The sky was clear and there was no wind. I didn't want to venture too far from the house, so I paced in her driveway and out into the cul-de-sac.

I started crying, sobbing really. It was the first time that I'd really cried since this whole ordeal began. I was feeling agitated and unsettled. My hands were trembling. My heart was racing.

I raised my trembling hands up and shouted, "You better not make a liar out of me! Don't make a liar out of me!"

All of a sudden, boom!

A large branch fell out of the tree that was near her driveway and landed at my feet.

I stood there looking at the branch at my feet and then up at the tree.

"Okay, so this is how you prove your presence and answer prayer!" I said out loud.

I reached down, picked up the branch, and carried it with me as I paced some more. Each time I walked past the tree, I looked up at it, trying to see where the branch broke off. The tree looked pristine. There was no evidence of where the branch used to be. I realized that there was no reason for this branch to have fallen at my feet. No reason at all, except by the grace of God.

I shook my head, and looking up, I said, "Thanks for your love and presence in all this mess!"

I carried the branch into the house and when mom woke up, I told her what happened and showed her the branch.

Handing her the branch, I said. "Mom, I prayed for you to have peace, for God to show you in a tangible way that God is with you now, that you are loved, and that there is nothing to fear. God answered my prayer by throwing this branch at me."

We sat together for a while, not saying anything, as Mom cradled the branch to her chest.

WIGIAT? God is present in our doubts and fears. God's presence gives us the courage to verbalize our questions, to ponder out loud. God is present in the comforting words of scripture, our book of faith. God is present in caring conversations and in the silence of our thoughts. God is present in the wailing and in the pacing. God is present in a branch falling from a tree. God is present in the surprising ways that prayer is answered. God is present.

CHAPTER 13
The Shower

It was increasingly difficult for Mom to get in and out of bed, so she was receiving sponge baths from the hospice aide. In my experience, these are often very unsettling and unsatisfying. You're exposed in your bed while the one who is bathing you does what needs to be done or helps you do the same. Like most people, Mom hated sponge baths!

Because getting in and out of bed was such a challenge, Mom also needed a catheter. The prolonged use of one made her uncomfortable and sore. I suspected that she hated it as much or more than the sponge baths!

Mom was weary, weary from sponge baths, weary from the catheter, and weary from being in the bed all day and all night long. She desperately wanted some normalcy, so one night while Jen and I were both at

On the Way . . .

her house she insisted upon getting out of bed and taking a shower.

Concerned, Jenny said, "The shower is at the other end of the house, you'll get super tired just getting there and back."

I added, "You might fall in the slippery shower and hurt yourself. Plus, if you fall, we won't be able to get you back up."

Mom rejected both of our objections and continued to push for a shower. She was hard-headed about things. Once she got an idea in her head, she wouldn't let it go until she got what she wanted. On top of that, once she decided that this was what she wanted, she wanted it right now.

She promised to be careful and she promised to let us help her. We recognized that we would be unable to change her mind, we relented. Thankfully, she allowed us to make some preparations before we got started.

Jen cleared the way between the family room where her bed was to the shower in her bedroom, picking up things that were on the floor and moving any furniture that might be a trip hazard.

I focused on getting the bathroom ready. I placed a towel, wash cloth, and clean pajamas in easy reach. I put her walker near the bathroom door since the wheelchair wouldn't fit through the doorway. We increased the heat in the house, so she wouldn't get cold.

I tried one more time to change her mind. "Mom, your aide is coming tomorrow. Let's wait for her to help you in the shower, Okay?"

She looked at me with stern eyes and in a strong voice said, "Get me to the shower."

We got her out of the bed and into her wheelchair. Jenny went ahead of us to turn on the shower so that the water could warm up. Then she met us at the bathroom door. With me stabilizing the wheelchair, she helped Mom stand up. Slowly, using her walker, Mom made her way to the running shower, first standing between the two of us so we could help her undress.

Then, Jenny exclaimed, "She can't stand in the shower by herself!"

Without hesitation, Jenny stepped into the running shower with her clothes on. I helped mom step in after her.

On the Way...

All of a sudden Mom declared, "Get this thing (reaching for her catheter) out of me!"

Hearing Mom demand to have her catheter out made getting her in the shower seem like a casual walk in the park! Neither Jenny nor I had any medical training beyond basic first aid and CPR. Removing a catheter was not something either of us wanted or were prepared to do!

"Mom," I said, "I don't know how to do that."

"If you don't take it out, I'll pull it out," Mom said as she attempted to reach down to grab the tubing.

I continued, "Mom, wait a minute. Pulling it out yourself will certainly hurt you. Let's get your shower finished and get you back to bed."

Mom repeated, "Get this thing out of me or I'll pull it out myself!"

Now Jenny chimed in, "Mom, you're standing naked in the shower. You're slippery and I'm afraid that you'll fall. Let's finish this shower."

Mom was even more forceful, "Call the nurse right now and have her come here to take this thing out. I want it out now."

So, I called the nurse. I filled her in on what was happening and asked her advice about what to do. She explained that she couldn't come right then.

The nurse was reluctant to tell me how to remove the catheter because I'm sure she picked up on how anxious I was. After listening to me and hearing Mom complain in the background, she realized that for Mom's well-being, and ours, we needed to remove it.

The nurse finally said, "You can take it out."

"Oh no, I'm not a nurse. I don't want to do this," I replied.

The nurse explained, "If she pulls it out, she will injure herself and be in a lot of pain. We can't let that happen. I'll tell you how to take it out."

After a deep sigh, I agreed, "Oh my. Okay. Tell me how."

The nurse explained how the catheter works. She told me about the balloon that holds it in place, saying "all you need to do is pop the balloon and then pull it out."

Sounds easy enough, right? Back to the bathroom I went, scissors in hand.

On the Way...

Mom was sitting on the little stoop in the shower and Jenny was standing beside her, both wet from the running shower. I explained what the nurse said to Mom and Jenny. Then asked Mom if she still wanted the catheter out. Silly me, of course she did.

Jenny helped her stand up again and I got on the floor of the shower with a pair of scissors. The water was still running so that Mom wouldn't get cold. With water splashing on my face, I looked up between her legs and tugged on the catheter line until I could see the balloon. Then I had second thoughts.

"Jenny," I said, "professionals usually do this while the patient is laying down. Are you sure we should do this? Are you . . .?"

Mom interrupted me, "Just get it over with!"

Before I began, I gave some instructions, "Jenny, hold on tight to Mom. Mom, please be still."

I tugged on the line again and revealed the balloon. Taking careful aim with the scissors, I poked the balloon to deflate it, and then pulled the catheter out.

Mom expressed her relief with an audible sigh. Now all three of us were soaking wet. Our relief turned to laughter as we realized what we had done and how silly we looked.

Mom said, "Well this is not something I ever expected my daughters to be doing with me!"

We agreed.

I slid out from under mom's legs and got up off the floor. Jenny turned off the water and then we helped mom step out of the shower. We moved her to the closed toilet where she could sit while she dried off. With some assistance she put clean underwear and pajamas. Then we helped her back to the wheelchair and headed back up the hallway to her bed.

Relaxed from the warm shower, in clean clothes, and exhausted from all the activity, Mom quickly drifted off to sleep.

In this situation, caring for Mom stretched us way beyond our comfort zones, beyond what we thought we were capable of doing. Because we loved Mom, we decided to do what she wanted even though it terrified us.

Wet and exhausted from all the effort, we were proud of ourselves for successfully meeting her needs that night.

On the Way . . .

Jenny went home to change and sleep in her own bed. I changed into some dry clothes and stayed at Mom's. It wasn't long before she woke up and told me that she'd had an accident in the bed. All I could do was shake my head. I helped her get out of bed so that I could change her sheets and put her in some clean clothes.

While she was sitting in the wheelchair she said, "I guess taking the catheter out wasn't such a good idea."

"You think?" Mom and I both laughed a little, then Mom asked me to call the nurse first thing in the morning so that she could put the catheter back in when she came for her visit. Of course, I would.

Before I drifted off to sleep, I took time to give thanks for mom's support team, the people who were on the way with us every day. "The Brain" couldn't care for Mom without each other's support. We couldn't care for Mom without the support of the hospice team. And we couldn't care for mom without the support of other friends and family members. You've heard the adage, "it takes a village to raise a child," I believe that this adage also applies to caring for a loved one in hospice.

WIGIAT? God was present in the teamwork that Jenny and I displayed that night. God was present in the cleansing water of the shower. God's presence gave us the courage to tackle the task that night, and God's presence kept mom safe. God was present in the hospice nurse who gave me the instructions I needed to respond to Mom's needs. God was present in the good night of sleep that followed. God was present.

CHAPTER 14
A Visit from Daddy

As Mom faced her own death, Daddy and his death came up often in conversation.

Growing weaker every day, it became even more difficult for Mom to move between her favorite well-worn recliner and her hospital bed. Mom spent a good bit of time in her chair one evening which she really enjoyed. But, when it was time to go to bed, she couldn't get up from the chair without help.

Jenny and I tried to help her. We got on each side of her so that we can help her stand up. She was too weak to help us, so this didn't work. We were afraid that we might hurt her or cause her to fall so we stopped trying.

Thankfully, the hospice nurse had mentioned, on an earlier visit, that the fire department would come and

On the Way...

physically move hospice patients if it was needed. Over Mom's objections, and seeing this as our only option, we called the non-emergency number and asked for their assistance.

Within a relatively short time, several firefighters arrived at her house. They were kind and gentle as they took the opportunity to chat with Mom for a few minutes. This put her at ease. With her consent one of them picked her up, cradled her like a baby, and placed her in the bed. It was a precious yet upsetting sight.

After they left, Mom enjoyed bragging about having her own firemen at her beck and call. This gave us a good laugh.

Late in the afternoon the next day, Mom was resting in her bed with her youngest granddaughter, Maggie, sitting nearby in Mom's recliner. I was in the kitchen cleaning up and preparing for dinner. The house was quiet.

Maggie walked up behind me and tapped me on the shoulder. She motioned for me to come into the family room. I followed her there and saw Mom sitting up in bed.

Mom hadn't moved or talked much since the fireman placed her in the bed the night before, so seeing her sitting up was startling.

I asked Maggie, "Did you help her sit up?"

Maggie said, "No, she just sat up by herself."

Looking up and into a far corner of the room Mom said, "Where have you been?"

Maggie and I exchanged glances with each other but didn't answer the question because it was apparent that she wasn't talking to us.

Mom continued, "Why did you leave me?"

Now it's clear that she was talking to my Dad. Her face was peaceful, and her voice was calm.

She said, "Come sit with me."

Then, without help, she turned, adjusted her position, and pated the bed.

While rubbing the sheet, she said, "I've missed you."

Silence filled the room, and then Mom said, "I'll see you soon."

On the Way . . .

She looked up to the corner again, a faint smile crossed her face. She adjusted her position and then laid back down. Her eyes continued to look up at the corner of the ceiling, her breathing was calm and steady.

Maggie and I looked at each other with tears flowing down our faces.

Maggie asked, "What just happened?"

"Your Granddaddy just came for a visit," I explained.

Maggie said, "But he died a long time ago,"

"You're right," I said, "He died long before you were born. We just witnessed him coming to comfort Grammy."

I continued, "There's a thin veil between our physical, earthly life and life after death. Every now and then we are blessed with an encounter where this veil opens up. This just happened." Being in the presence of the holy that day was a powerful experience.

The exchange we witnessed between Mom and Dad was the last time that we heard Mom speak.

I glanced at Mom, she had drifted off to sleep, more peacefully then she had been able to do in a long time.

I got a deep sense that her death was approaching so we called the rest of the family and encouraged them to come.

Mom looked uncomfortable in the bed, so Maggie and I decided to adjust her position. This time, moving her around didn't agitate or disturb her sleep like it had done in the past. Placing the blanket around her, we tucked her in and let her rest.

In this encounter with the holy, our compassionate God gave Mom the gift of a visit from Dad, the love of her life, to prepare her for the movement from physical life to eternal life.

Thankfully, this gift was intended for us as well. Maggie and I were blessed to experience this breakthrough moment, this thin place where the veil opens, and heaven and earth exist in the same space.

Having been witnesses to this made it possible for us to recall the experience for others which provided comfort and hope in the face of her death.

On the Way...

WIGIAT? God's presence was made known in the strong and loving arms of a fireman who moved Mom back into her bed. God's presence created the thin place where Mom was blessed with a holy visit with my dad, who had preceded her in death many years before. God was present in that break-through moment offering peace and assurance that all was well and will continue to be well as Mom prepared to be on her way one last time. God was present.

CHAPTER 15
The Final Hours

After Dad's visit, Mom settled into a deep sleep in her bed. She looked peaceful. There was no sign of pain in her facial expression and her body looked comfortable. Looking at her gave us peace because it was so clear that she was not suffering at all.

She was breathing more slowly than before. I recognized this as one of the indicators that death was coming near.

The reality is that you don't know when natural death will occur, when that last breath will be taken. All you have are signs which indicate that the time of death is approaching. From slower breathing and a slower pulse rate, from a purplish color of her hands and feet to a blotchy look to her arms and legs, the transition from the earthly life into the life to come was taking place.

On the Way...

With the family on the way, I continued my work preparing dinner. Maggie helped a little but preferred to sit with her Grammy. We prepared a table in another room so that we could all be together for dinner. We shared stories and memories, which triggered laughter and tears. Sitting there together we recognized that soon the matriarch of our family would no longer be physically with us.

Christian worship was important to Mom and our family. As the time of her death approached, it seemed that this was what we should do after dinner. Our friend, CJ, played the piano, so we invited her over to help us sing some of Mom's favorite worship songs.

Gathering in the family room with Mom, we sang. "Amazing Grace," "You Have Come Down to the Lakeshore," "Here I Am, Lord;" "Surely the Presence of the Lord is in This Place," and many others.

The way that Mom lived her life reminded me of the story of Martha and Mary from Luke, chapter 10. I reflected on this with the family.

At times in her life, Mom was Martha. Busy in the kitchen taking care of whatever needed to be done. Preparing food and drinks for community meals, hosting dinner parties and other gatherings were ways that Mom showed her love to others. Sometimes, she was even cranky, like Martha, complaining when she felt like she was working harder than others. But most of the time she took pride in her efforts to provide the best possible experience for her guests. Generosity and hospitality were two of Mom's greatest gifts which she used to their fullest potential.

At other times, Mom was Mary. She loved reading and studying her bible. Participating in Sunday school classes and other opportunities to deepen her faith were important to her. She organized her life around worship, activities at her church, and opportunities to care for others. Even after Daddy's death, while her world was in chaos, Mom's faith remained central to how she journeyed through life. This was and is a beautiful witness to those who love her.

Receiving Holy Communion was a meaningful aspect of worship for Mom. In earlier conversation, Mom mentioned that she felt closest to Daddy while receiving communion. This isn't an unusual comment about the impact of sharing in the Lord's Supper. Communion is often described as a place where the thin veil that divides our physical life from eternal life opens for a moment as we join with all the saints at the great feast.

On the Way...

We continued to sit with Mom that night, singing songs, reading scripture, sharing stories and memories. Then we shared holy communion together. Communing someone who is unresponsive is a holy experience. I took the consecrated wafer, dipped it into the consecrated wine, and rubbed it across my Mom's lips. Instinctively, she licked her lips and received the body and blood of Jesus, her Lord. Then I ate the wafer on her behalf.

Clinging to these precious moments in silence was the only thing that we could do. CJ played music on her keyboard and we sat together for a while, sometimes singing softly, sometimes chatting quietly, and sometimes just being with her, together. Eventually, the mood shifted, and we returned to normal voices and regular routines. There were dishes to clean and a house to tidy up.

We took turns sitting near Mom, holding her hand, rubbing her feet, and speaking to her until she drew her final breath and died peacefully at 2:47 a.m. on Saturday, November 17, 2008.

WIGIAT? God's presence was everywhere that day. With the family that gathered and the stories and memories we shared. With the laughter and tears that flowed freely. God's presence touched us in tangible ways as we sang, prayed, and communed together, right there with Mom. God's presence escorted Mom home and remained with us as we said our good-byes.

CHAPTER 16
The Days After

Sitting with Mom after her death was bittersweet. We were thankful that her long struggle was over. It had been four months since her cancer diagnosis and two months in hospice care. We were deeply sad. Our Mom and Grammy was no longer with us. We missed her laughter and playfulness, we missed her generous spirit and gracious hospitality, we missed her direct nature and her quickness to express love.

Recalling the times and adventures we shared with her made us nostalgic. We pulled out all of the pictures we could find of her life and enjoyed looking through them. Each one told a story; some we knew and, sadly, some we didn't.

On the Way...

Making the necessary phone calls was tedious as we reported her death to hospice, doctors, family and friends, the church, cemetery, and the Cremation Society. The hospice nurse came over to do the final exam and made the declaration of death. The hospice aide came to bathe and dress her. But to her surprise, Jenny and I had already done this.

It was precious work. We bathed her, put lotion all over her body, combed her hair, and dressed her in a favorite dress. Handling her body in this way helped us feel an intense connection with her. It was holy ground.

The hardest part of this day was the arrival of the Cremation Society to pick up her body. Someone had been by her side since she died. The thought of her being alone now was unbearable. The attendants who came to pick her up were compassionate and kind. With much care, they moved her to a gurney and then draped her body with a cloth. This sight was hard for all of us. It brought me to tears, sobbing tears.

That was the moment when the reality of her death hit hard. She would not be coming back to this house. She would no longer sit in her chair, walk down the hall, turn on her favorite lamp, drink from her favorite coffee cup. She was dead.

We watched as they put the gurney in the hearse, closed the door, and drove away.

Now what? Because we hadn't slept in over 24 hours, we decided to head to our homes to rest, promising to come together the next day to figure everything out.

There were decisions to make and things to do. The Cremation Society provided us with a helpful checklist that outlined the legal things we needed to do. We coordinated with the church for the memorial service, with the cemetery for the burial, and with the Cremation Society for a small visitation before she was cremated. This allowed us to see her one more time.

Exhaustion and grief made for an interesting combination. Sometimes we were laughing uncontrollably and other times we couldn't stop crying. We spent a lot of time at Mom's house sorting through piles and piles of paper, looking for information about life insurance policies, documentation about her pensions and social security.

To our surprise Laura found the title to Mom's car stuck between the pages of a magazine, an old and generic magazine. With this in hand, Jenny and I decided to go ahead and sell her car. We drove it to a dealership and, thankfully, they purchased it from us. This gave us some cash. Rather than putting it away for expenses related to settling her affairs, we decided to spend it. Something Mom would have done!

We gathered the five granddaughters and the seven of us went to one of Mom's favorite stores where we each purchased a new outfit to wear to the memorial service. Mom loved bright colors and flashy clothes, so we decided that we'd look for outfits that matched her style and that made us feel comfortable. This shopping spree was therapeutic for everyone. We encouraged and helped each other find just the right outfit. Mom would have enjoyed this experience so much!

The birthday for Jenny's middle daughter, Abi, was just four days after Mom's death. Rather than delay a family birthday celebration, we decided to eat together at one of Mom's favorite places. It seemed fitting to acknowledge that life and death are natural parts of our existence as human beings. Gathered together we gave thanks for Abi and for Mom as we enjoyed that time together.

On the day of Mom's memorial service, we gathered at the church to greet friends before the service. It was such a blessing to see so many of her friends all together in one place. We held the service that Mom designed in exactly the way that she wanted with lots of joyous singing. I'm sure that she would've loved it!

After the service, we made our way to the cemetery where Mom's cremains would be laid to rest in her own grave right beside Daddy. The closest she'd been to him in a long, long time. After the committal, the family went to a local restaurant to eat. This gave the cemetery time to do what they needed to do with her grave. After a while we headed back and gathered around her grave. The cemetery had placed the flowers from the service on her grave which made it so beautiful.

Prior to Mom's cremation, I asked the funeral home to set aside some of her cremains for me which they did. I placed the container in a small box so I that they'd be less visible. Remember, Mom expressed a desire to be buried in the same grave as my Dad, but the cemetery said that it wasn't possible. Little did they know, I'd find a way to carry out her request.

Gathered around her grave, I told the family about Grammy's wish and what the cemetery had said. Then explained that I had a little shovel with me so that we could make it happen. Thankfully, I realized that seeing cremains for the first time, especially of

On the Way...

someone you love, is extremely hard. So, before I opened the box, I explained what we'd see and encouraged those who might be uncomfortable to wait near the car.

We knew that the cemetery wouldn't be happy with us if they knew what we were about to do, so we had several people posted as look outs. They were to let us know if anyone from the cemetery headed our way.

We moved to stand around Daddy's grave. I took the little shovel and dug a shallow trench in the ground above his casket. Then, I poured Mom's cremains into the trench, spreading them out, working them into the dirt. We covered the cremains with the dirt and grass that I had removed while digging the trench. Looking at each other, we felt a sense of accomplishment because we had met Mom's desire to be buried with the love of her life in the best way possible.

Being sneaky and breaking the rules caused us to have a much-needed laugh. Mom would've been so proud!

WIGIAT? God's presence was experienced through the unexpected laughter and joy that happened as we shopped and enjoyed a birthday meal together. God was present in the loving support we received from friends, family, the church community, the Cremation Society, and the cemetery. God's presence was evident in all the people who came to celebrate her life. God's presence comforted us as we gathered around the graves of both my parents, gave thanks for their lives, and saw them united again at last.

PART TWO

Biblical Reflections on Caring for a Loved One in Hospice

*Reflection on
1 Corinthians 13:4-8, 13*

---

[4]Love is patient; love is kind; love is not envious or boastful or arrogant [5]or rude. It does not insist on its own way; it is not irritable or resentful; [6]it does not rejoice in wrong doing, but rejoices in the truth. [7]It bears all things, believes all things, hopes all things, endures all things. [8]Love never ends. [13]And now faith, hope, and love abide, these three; and the greatest of these is love.

Mom loved to hear this passage read because it reminded her of the love she shared with my Dad and the enormity of God's love. Maybe it will speak to you as well about who God is, how God is present in your circumstance, and how this description of love can shape your relationships with others.

On the Way...

When you are weary and wonder where God is in all that is happening, this passage can remind you of God's character. The Greek word for love here is *agape*. It describes the unconditional love of God. In 1 John 4:8, we're told that "God is love." If God is love, then God is patient, kind, not envious or boastful or arrogant or rude. God doesn't rejoice in wrongdoing but rejoices in the truth.

God doesn't rejoice in your weariness and in the disease that is plaguing your loved one. God doesn't rejoice in the sadness you feel or in the loss of life that you are anticipating. Instead God rejoices in the truth. And the truth is that God bears all things, believes all things, endures all things.

Beloved, know that God is present in whatever circumstance you are facing today. God is supporting you, bearing all things with you, enduring all things on your behalf.

Because God is patient and kind, you need never worry about God's deep and abiding love for you and those you love.

This passage is often used in wedding services because those getting married aspire to the fullness of love that is described in these verses. But living out love in this way, every day, is incredibly hard. We found that to be true while we cared for mom.

When things are going smoothly, it's easy to be patient, kind, not envious, boastful, arrogant, or rude. It's easy to avoid insisting on your own way or being irritable or resentful. When things are going well, when you are rested and at peace, it's easy to see the presence of God in the actions of others.

But when things are stressful, when emotions are raw, when you're on edge wondering when the end will come, your capacity to demonstrate patience and kindness is challenged. Lack of sleep and less than healthy eating habits can cause you to be irritable and resentful.

Remember that this is a difficult time and be gentle with yourself and others. When you feel yourself slipping into behaviors that aren't helpful, find a way to take a break: take a walk, take a nap, grab something to eat, take a moment to rest in God's enduring love.

Paul wrote, "And now faith, hope, and love abide, these three, and the greatest of these is love." Faith is the gift that God gives to us in this life so that we can trust in the mercy and love of God. Hope is the gift that enables us to wait for the fulfillment of God's

On the Way...

promises. It's faith and hope that turn our eyes to the future where there will be no more tears, no more crying, and no more pain. We need both faith and hope in this life when there is so much pain and suffering.

But once we die, once the promises of God are fulfilled for us in death, we no longer need faith and hope. These have served us well while we were alive. In death, we are gathered into the fullness of God's love. In death, love is all there is because God is love.

Beloved, rest in the faith and hope that is yours today because they are gifts from God. Let the presence of Love hold you tightly. Let Love fill you with peace.

Loving God,

Thank you for your deep love for me and for those I love. Help me to reflect your love to others in all that I do and say today. Guide me by your Spirit so that I will be patient and kind in every interaction. When I am weary, keep me from being envious, arrogant, resentful, boastful, irritable, and rude. Surround me with your love as I walk through this difficult time. Thank you for bearing all things, believing all things, hoping all things, and enduring all things, on my behalf. Sustain my faith, restore my hope, and draw me into your love. Amen.

Reflection on Colossians 3:12-14

> *^{12}As God's chosen ones, holy and beloved, clothe yourselves with compassion, kindness, humility, meekness, and patience. ^{13}Bear with one another and, if anyone has a complaint against another, forgive each other; just as the Lord has forgiven you, so you also must forgive. ^{14}Above all, clothe yourselves with love, which binds everything together in perfect harmony.*

Caregiving is extremely hard work, especially when it's a 24-hour a day task. Even when you're not "on duty" you're likely to worry about your loved one and those who are providing care in your absence. Thoughts about them and concern for their well-being make care giving exhausting!

In this passage, Paul reminds us who we are: God's chosen ones, holy and beloved. You, my friend, are

On the Way...

God's chosen one, holy and blameless. God chose you before the foundations of the world (Ephesians 1:4). You belong to God and you are deeply loved as a child of God.

We're told to put on compassion, kindness, humility, meekness, and patience. These are traits we need when we interact with and care for each other. When you have to put something on, it means that you aren't already wearing it. Clothing ourselves with these virtues may not come naturally to us especially when we're going through challenging times where our emotional, spiritual, and physical well-being are stretched to their limits.

Putting on compassion, kindness, humility, meekness, and patience is an intentional decision we need to make every day. They are life-giving and build relationships rather than tear them down. Wearing compassion, kindness, humility, meekness, and patience enables us respond to each other from a place of love and grace rather than frustration and anger.

Paul, then, turns his attention to how we are to behave around each other. He says, "¹³Bear with one another and, if anyone has a complaint against another, forgive each other; just as the Lord has forgiven you, so you also must forgive."

When you're exhausted, worried, and preoccupied it can become challenging to bear with one another. Your emotions may be raw, and your thoughts may be jumbled—this is the reason that being intentional about wearing those traits that are life-giving is so important. Beloved, acknowledge your feelings, your jumbled thoughts, your confusion and pain. Share them with those you love. Seek their forgiveness when you need to and when they ask for your forgiveness, grant it graciously.

This is what love is all about. Clothing yourself with love enables you to bear with one another, it enables you to seek and grant forgiveness. It enables you to demonstrate compassion, kindness, humility, meekness, and patience when things are going well and when things are not going the way you'd like them to go.

The love that binds everything together in perfect harmony is God's love. Lean in to that love and let God's love empower your interactions with the one you are caring for and all those you love.

On the Way...

Loving God,

Clothe me with your love and help me to put on compassion, kindness, humility, meekness, and patience in all of my interactions today. Enable me to bear with those I love when things are going well and when things are stressed and uncertain. Let your love bring harmony and peace into every interaction. Amen.

Reflection on Ecclesiastes 3:1-8

---

*¹For everything there is a season,
and a time for every matter under heaven:
²a time to be born, and a time to die;
a time to plant, and a time to
pluck up what is planted;
³a time to kill, and a time to heal;
a time to break down, and a time to build up;
⁴a time to weep, and a time to laugh;
a time to mourn, and a time to dance;
⁵a time to throw away stones,
and a time to gather stones together;
a time to embrace, and a time
to refrain from embracing;
⁶a time to seek, and a time to lose;
a time to keep, and a time to throw away;
⁷a time to tear, and a time to sew;
a time to keep silence, and a time to speak;
⁸a time to love, and a time to hate;
a time for war, and a time for peace.*

On the Way . . .

In one sentence, the writer of Ecclesiastes named how fragile human life is as he named the dichotomy of life and death. We all walk that same path, we've been born and with each day we get closer to death. Death is a reality shared by every human being. Most of us aren't aware that death is approaching sooner rather than later. But a person under hospice care knows that they are more rapidly approaching the moment of death.

My mother was ready to die. The only thing she feared about death was the physical pain that might be associated with it. Thankfully, her hospice nurse was able to manage her pain well. The truth is that she couldn't control the time of her death. What she could control was how she continued to live while she was dying.

I love how this poem names a wide variety of seasons in our lives. So often we get caught up in the chronological way of thinking about time: morning, mid-day, afternoon, evening, night time; days, weeks, months, years; fall, winter, spring, summer; moving from one appointment to another. When we organize our lives in that way, we can miss the important moments of life.

The writer of Ecclesiastes is challenging us to avoid marking time through our calendars and instead focus on relationships. These pairings are less about a particular time and more about a particular way of being in the world. A particular way of being in relationship with those around us, with creation, and with God.

The dying process is in God's time. We don't get the details ahead of time. What we do get are the seasons and times for every matter under heaven. The reality is that none of these seasons and times last forever. Maybe that's good news. Maybe that's what helps us persevere through the times of sorrow, hardship, and pain because we know that joy comes in the morning. Grace follows hardship, peace follows anxiety, and healing follows sickness. The key then is to live in the present moment, in the best way possible.

In what season and time are you today? Is now a time to weep or a time to laugh? Is now a time to mourn or a time to dance? Is today a time to keep silence or a time to speak? Is today a time to embrace or a time to refrain from embracing?

In whatever season you are right now, know that it's okay. That God is there with you. Live in your time and don't hold back. Laugh when you want to laugh.

On the Way...

Weep when you need to weep. Mourn when your heart and mind bring you to that place. Dance when the Spirit causes you to move. Keep silence when you need that space to rest, to ponder all that is happening around you. Speak the words you long to say, words of appreciation, words of hope and love. Embrace yourself and the ones around you. Refrain from embracing when you need to be in your own space, in your own thoughts.

Beloved, there are no right or wrong ways to move through this time, this season of your life. That is the blessing of this passage. The key is to keep on living in the moment of where you are and how you're feeling. Give grace to the others in your life so that they too can live in their moment without fear and anxiety.

May the God of all time grant you to laugh, weep, mourn, dance, keep silence, speak, embrace, and refrain from embrace in ways that bring comfort and peace during this season of your life.

Ever-present God,

Thank you for your presence in every moment of my life today. Let that presence be known in tangible ways. Comfort me as I move through the ups and downs of life. Remind me that the only thing that lasts forever is your love. Set me free from fear and anxiety and empower me to live in each moment of every day during this season and time of my life. Amen.

Reflection on Ephesians 3:14-16

¹⁴For this reason I bow my knees before the Father, ¹⁵from whom every family in heaven and on earth takes its name. ¹⁶I pray that, according to the riches of his glory, he may grant that you may be strengthened in your inner being with power through his Spirit, ¹⁷and that Christ may dwell in your hearts through faith, as you are being rooted and grounded in love. ¹⁸I pray that you may have the power to comprehend, with all the saints, what is the breadth and length and height and depth, ¹⁹and to know the love of Christ that surpasses knowledge, so that you may be filled with all the fullness of God.

Comprehending the love of God has been and continues to be challenging for all the saints, those who've gone before us, those among us now,

On the Way . . .

and those coming after us. We've all been taught to be suspicious of anything that sounds too good to be true, this includes the unconditional love of God.

This prayer of Paul is a blessing for us because it acknowledges the reality of our own struggles and connects us to the struggles of believers throughout the centuries. The only antidote to this struggle, to our lack of comprehension, is the power that comes through the Holy Spirit and the presence of Christ dwelling in us.

Paul prays that we will be "strengthened in our inner being." So often we make trusting God a head thing. Something that we have to understand completely by professing right doctrine, quoting the right bible verses, being certain of everything as it relates to God and us. This way of being a faithful follower of Jesus will only frustrate you. It will lead you to feelings of unworthiness and inadequacy.

"Strengthening in our inner being" happens in our gut, it happens in our spirit. It takes us out of our heads and into the depths of who we are. Paul prays for the power of the Spirit and the indwelling of Christ to root and ground us in love.

Notice that this is happening *to* us, not *by* us. Let this free you from any expectation that you are going to figure out this God thing by yourself. You simply can't. You can try really hard, you can go to worship every Sunday, read your Bible every day, pray all the time, and be kind to your neighbor but you are going to fall short. Don't get me wrong, these are all faithful things to do, faithful actions of a follower of Jesus. We do them, not to gain favor with God, but in response to the riches of God's glory, in thankfulness for God's love.

All of this is for the purpose of helping us comprehend the wideness and fullness of the love of Christ. This love of Christ enables us to persevere through the ups and downs of life. This love of Christ receives our doubts and our questions, receives our anxiety and our fears.

Beloved, rest in that love. Rest in the fullness of God, who is holding you today, not expecting anything from you in return. Let this love strengthen and ground you in the fullness of God.

Gracious God,

Your love is deeper and wider than I can ever understand. Send forth your Spirit to strengthen me for all that I am experiencing today. Deepen my faith

On the Way...

in you and dispel my doubts and fears. Enfold me in the fullness of your love. Amen.

Reflection on Hebrews 12:1-3

---

¹Therefore, since we are surrounded by so great a cloud of witnesses, let us also lay aside every weight and the sin that clings so closely, and let us run with perseverance the race that is set before us, ²looking to Jesus the pioneer and perfecter of our faith, who for the sake of the joy that was set before him endured the cross, disregarding its shame, and has taken his seat at the right hand of the throne of God.

You, beloved, are surrounded by this great cloud of witnesses. A cloud that includes those you've loved who are already at rest and those who are surrounding you right now. It includes all the witnesses you've not met personally but who, through their witness, revealed God's love to you. This great cloud of witnesses includes Abraham and Sarah,

On the Way...

Moses, Aaron, and Miriam; David and Deborah; Naomi and Rachel; Mary, the mother of Jesus and Mary of Magdala; Mary and Martha; Peter, James, John, and all of the disciples; it includes Paul, Peter, and Timothy; Phoebe, Lydia, and Dorcus. We give thanks for them and the depth of their witness.

When we think of the witnesses of days gone by, we can cling to the promise that they are in the presence of God. Gathered with all the saints, they unite their voices in worship and prayer around the throne of God. They ran their race, looking to Jesus who was the pioneer and perfector of their faith, and are at rest in the house of the Lord. This is what awaits your loved one and all the rest of us who are living now.

Recognizing the witnesses of days gone by is comforting, maybe even powerful, but it may not be enough to carry you through the ups and downs of life. The truth is that you need witnesses you can touch and see. Witnesses who can hold you tightly, hold your hand, give you a hug, speak actual words of encouragement and comfort to you. Witnesses who will show up to pray, sing, laugh, and cry with you. Witnesses who will point you to Jesus, who will be Jesus with skin on.

The witnesses in the great cloud, showed us how they lived faithfully in their own brokenness. None of them was perfect. They all made mistakes, they all fell short. Thankfully, their presence in the cloud of witnesses had nothing to do with who they were or how they lived their life. Their presence is all because of Jesus. His redemptive love gathered them into the cloud.

The same is true for the witnesses who are living among us now. True for you and me. None of us is perfect. We all make mistakes. We all fall short. And just like the witnesses of days gone by, our presence in the cloud of witnesses has nothing to do with who we are or how we live our life. Our presence in the cloud is all because of Jesus. His redemptive love gathers us into the cloud.

This is what it means to name Jesus as the pioneer and perfector of our faith. This is a powerful description of who Jesus is and what Jesus accomplishes in his life, death, and resurrection.

Jesus, the Word made flesh, full of grace and truth, is the only completely faithful one. He pointed to God as the source of his ability to heal and perform miracles. His trust in the Father, took him to the cross and into the grave where he waited for God to

On the Way...

claim ultimate victory over sin, death, and the power of the devil in his resurrection.

We are yoked to the faithfulness of Jesus. It's his faith that makes us right with God. It's his faith that makes our relationship with God possible. Without Jesus, our faithfulness is always going to be flawed. We pray for God's intervention in our lives and then continue worrying. We spin our wheels trying to figure out what to do in a situation and forget to seek God's guidance. Thanks be to God, for the gift of Jesus who perfects our faith, who makes our faithfulness complete.

This is what enables us to run with perseverance the race of life. This race is not a sprint, that we run as fast as we can. Instead, the race of life is a marathon. A race that we run one moment, one day, at a time. We can't run this race by ourselves. Of course, we try, we try to do life on our own. But, by ourselves, we don't have the stamina to complete the race.

Surrounded by the great cloud of witnesses, we know that we're not alone. And with Jesus as the pioneer and perfector of our faith, we are empowered, enabled, to run the race. This is the true gift of community. None of us can do life on our own, not even Jesus. He surrounded himself with a community of people who journeyed with him. They provided companionship as he walked the way that was set before him.

Lean into the community that is surrounding you. Draw strength from the cloud of witnesses who are your companions in this season of your life. Draw courage and peace from Jesus whose faith carries you as you run with perseverance the race that is set before you.

Faithful God,

Thank you for the gift of community; for the great cloud of witnesses who reveal your love to me today. Thank you for the gift of Jesus whose faith makes it possible for me to persevere in this season of life. Grant me all that I need today to walk the way of faith. Amen.

Reflection on Isaiah 43:1-5a

---

^{1}But now thus says the LORD,
he who created you, O Jacob,
he who formed you, O Israel:
Do not fear, for I have redeemed you;
I have called you by name, you are mine.
^{2}When you pass through the waters,
I will be with you;
and through the rivers, they shall not overwhelm you;
when you walk through fire you shall not be burned,
and the flame shall not consume you.
^{3}For I am the LORD your God,
the Holy One of Israel, your Savior.
I give Egypt as your ransom,
Ethiopia and Seba in exchange for you.
^{4}Because you are precious in my sight,
and honored, and I love you,
I give people in return for you,
nations in exchange for your life.
^{5}Do not fear, for I am with you.

On the Way...

Facing a serious, life threatening illness has the potential to challenge all that we know about ourselves and the God who created us. We might wonder how this could be happening to our loved one. We might wonder where God is in all of this. These, and so many others, are normal questions when faced with a diagnosis that points to the death of a loved one.

Rest assured that whatever you are feeling today, right now, is normal. Your feelings are real, and they belong to you. If you can, avoid the temptation to compare what you're going through and what you're feeling to anyone else. Every illness, every diagnosis, every prognosis, every reaction is unique.

That's why this passage from Isaiah is so important. Here the Lord makes it clear that we are created, formed, and redeemed by the Lord, our God. And because we belong to God we need not live in fear. This message seems to be important to God because the phrase "do not fear" or don't be afraid" appears over and over again in the Old and New Testaments.

Throughout the biblical witness, the phrase "do not fear" or something similar is spoken to people in an effort to calm their troubled spirits, to cast out their doubt, and to assure them that they are safe in God's love.

In the midst of difficult things, it's really hard to avoid being afraid. Walking with Mom in hospice care filled us with fear, simply because it was new territory. We had not walked this way before, so the promise of God to be with us was comforting.

The same may be true for you. You may not have journeyed this road before. Every turn in the road is a surprise, every bump may rattle you to your core, you may face every hill and every valley with trepidation as you wait to see what will happen next.

Beloved, these are the promises of the Lord for you:

When you pass through the exhausting long days and sleepless dark nights, the Lord is with you.

When the challenges you face are overwhelming and the burdens you carry weigh you down, the Lord is with you.

When you're being asked to make decisions about things you know nothing about, the Lord is with you.

On the Way . . .

When there are medical challenges, financial hurdles, or your relationships with others are strained, the Lord is with you.

The Lord is always with you and will not abandon you. The emotional, mental, spiritual, physical pain you are experiencing will not consume you.

You can claim this promise because the Lord your God calls you by name and you belong to God. You, beloved, are precious in God's sight, honored and loved completely and without any hesitation on God's part.

This doesn't mean that this season of your life will be easy. It doesn't mean that grief and sorrow will not affect your life. We know that they will. Walking alongside and supporting a person who is dying is hard work.

Beloved, know that God is with you; God is for you. You're not going through this season alone. Rest in the presence of God and cling to God's promise to sustain you, for you are redeemed, called, claimed, precious, honored, and loved by the One who created and formed you.

Dear God,

Draw near to me as I journey through uncertain times. Hold me close. Guide me as I face whatever lies ahead of me today. Make your presence known to me in real and tangible ways so that I will not be afraid. Amen.

Reflection on Mark 2:1-5

---

¹When he returned to Capernaum after some days, it was reported that he was at home. ²So many gathered around that there was no longer room for them, not even in front of the door; and he was speaking the word to them. ³Then some people came, bringing to him a paralyzed man, carried by four of them. ⁴And when they could not bring him to Jesus because of the crowd, they removed the roof above him; and after having dug through it, they let down the mat on which the paralytic lay. ⁵When Jesus saw their faith, he said to the paralytic, "Son, your sins are forgiven."

In this interaction with Jesus we see the impact of friends in the life of a sick person. Without his

On the Way...

friends, the paralyzed man remained isolated from his community, unable to participate in everyday activities, unable to enjoy the company of others.

Without his friends, he remained confined to his mat. His world was limited to the four walls of his room. The rhythm of each sunrise and each sunset was lost as he laid endlessly upon his mat.

Without his friends, the paralyzed man would have missed the opportunity to see and be seen by Jesus. The crowds blocked his view and made it impossible for Jesus to even know of his presence, or of his need.

Beloved, what blocks your view of Jesus today? Is it the burden of caring for a loved one? Is it the exhaustion that comes from long days and nights? Is it your fear, your confusion, your doubt?

Now, I suspect that the crowds didn't intend to create a barrier between the paralyzed man and Jesus. They, too, simply wanted to be in the presence of Jesus.

Seeing the crowds that day, the friends could have turned around and gone home, but they refused to let the crowds stop them. Instead of giving up, they went up onto the roof.

Getting the man up on the roof was not enough. They had to dig through the thatched roof to create a hole big enough to get the man inside. Once the hole was large enough, they lowered the man down to the floor right in front of Jesus.

Jesus saw the tenacity of these friends and the extent of their effort to get the paralyzed man in his presence. Witnessing this, Jesus chose to announce forgiveness and healing for the paralyzed man.

Being a caregiver takes that same kind of tenacity. That same determination to care for the one you love and to care for yourself. Lots of obstacles and challenges will come your way during this caregiving journey. You and your loved one will need friends around you who will take risks for and with you, who will look out for you, and advocate for you.

One of the things that always stands out for me in this passage is the silence of the paralyzed man. It appears that he doesn't ask Jesus for anything, not for forgiveness and not for healing.

This is such Good News! Jesus announces forgiveness and healing without a confession of sin and without a pronouncement of faith. It's all about the love that Jesus has for the friends who risked everything for their loved one.

On the Way...

Later in this story, Jesus tells the paralytic to stand up, pick up his mat, and go home. Your loved one may not be able to physically stand and pick up their mat. That kind of healing may not be possible now but healing always happens when we are in the presence of Jesus. There will come a day when your loved one will be set free from the disease that is ending their life. When that day comes, they will stand up, pick up their mat, and join Jesus in the fullness of God's love fulfilled for them.

Beloved, Jesus is looking at you today in love and peace. Jesus knows the challenges that you are fighting to overcome and the risks that you're taking every day. Jesus sees your tenacity on behalf of your loved one and embraces you with unconditional love and mercy.

Forgiving God,

Thank you for looking with favor upon me and my loved one. Thank you for giving me the strength I need to overcome challenges and take risks to provide care to another person. Remind me that forgiveness and healing are mine not because of who I am, but because of who you are. Amen.

Reflection on Philippians 4:4-9

⁴Rejoice in the Lord always; again I will say, Rejoice. ⁵Let your gentleness be known to everyone. The Lord is near. ⁶Do not worry about anything, but in everything by prayer and supplication with thanksgiving let your requests be made known to God. ⁷And the peace of God, which surpasses all understanding, will guard your hearts and your minds in Christ Jesus.

⁸Finally, beloved, whatever is true, whatever is honorable, whatever is just, whatever is pure, whatever is pleasing, whatever is commendable, if there is any excellence and if there is anything worthy of praise, think about these things. ⁹Keep on doing the things that you have learned and received and heard and seen in me, and the God of peace will be with you.

On the Way...

Beloved, the Lord is near, already present in whatever circumstance, in whatever situation you are living in now, in whatever concern you are lifting up in prayer.

Therefore, Paul writes, rejoice always. This was an important message for the church at Philippi, facing all kinds of hardships, all kinds of struggles, just as it is for us today. We don't rejoice because life is easy. We rejoice because the Lord is near. We rejoice because we are not going through the difficult times in our lives alone.

And because the Lord is near, you need not worry about anything. This is not permission to just sit around twiddling your thumbs waiting for God to work everything out. Instead, knowing, believing, and trusting that the Lord is near is an antidote to worry. It's an antidote to the anxiety and fear that can, that does, paralyze you. Because the Lord is near, actively present in your life, worry doesn't have to control you, doesn't need to consume your thoughts.

Paul tells us that in EVERYTHING, in the good, the bad, and the ugly, in EVERYTHING by prayer and supplication, with thanksgiving, let your requests be made known to God.

Pam Northrup

In Everything—no scenario is outside of God's concern for you. No situation is too small. God wants to receive it all, to be near, is near in all of it, already.

This is the kind of relationship that God has with you. A relationship of presence, of love, of hope, not dependent on how good you are, or the words you use or the way you pray. God longs for you to be free of your burdens, your worry, and so gives to you the gift of prayer.

Paul says, by prayer and supplication, with thanksgiving—by prayer, let prayer, let abiding in Jesus, carry you through each moment of every day.

By supplication, a fancy word for asking, asking in everything, in every moment of concern, every moment of hope, every moment of worry, every moment of joy, every moment of sorrow, every moment of delight, every moment of pain, and every moment of pleasure—in every moment, ask.

With thanksgiving—giving thanks for God's presence already, giving thanks for the work that God has already done, is doing, and will continue to do

By prayer and supplication, with thanksgiving . . .

On the Way...

Let your requests be made known to God—your requests, that's a powerful word, a reminder that you're not in charge, you aren't in a position to tell God what to do—and so you are encouraged to make your requests known, to ask.

Ask for what you need, ask for relief from the burdens and concerns that weigh you down. Remember that nothing is too small, nothing is outside of God's concern for you.

And then there is this beautiful promise: Paul said, 'and the peace of God, which surpasses all understanding will guard your hearts and minds in Christ Jesus.'

When your focus is on the One who gives you the gift of prayer, on the One who is already present with you, on the One to whom you pray, God's peace is with you.

Notice that it's not your peace that comes to you. Paul doesn't say, "and the peace of you, which surpassing all understanding will guard your hearts and mind in Christ Jesus.'

Instead Paul is clear—it's the peace of God, the peace of God which holds you tightly, the peace of God which guards your heart and mind in Christ Jesus while you wait, while you pray, and while you live.

Our God is relational, one who is near to you right now. Therefore, Paul encourages us to focus on whatever is true, whatever is honorable, whatever is just, whatever is pure, whatever is pleasing, whatever is commendable. These are the good things, the blessings and gifts that God brings into your life.

Getting focused on the opposite of those values; shifting attention to whatever is false, whatever is shameful, whatever is unjust, whatever is tainted, whatever is unpleasant, and whatever is lamentable will separate you from God and from those around you. You'll get distracted and lose touch with what and who's important in your life.

The antidote to that is to think on the things that are worthy of praise, things that are life-giving and then rest in the God of peace who will be, who is always, with you.

God of peace,

Thank you for the gift of prayer. Thank you for the encouragement to bring my worries and concerns to

On the Way...

you. Take away the worry and concerns that weigh me down and let your peace dwell in my heart. Be present with me and those I love today. Turn my attention away from those things that separate me from you and from others. Draw me into the goodness of life with you and help me to rest in your peace. Amen.

Reflection on Psalm 6

¹O LORD, do not rebuke me in your anger, or discipline me in your wrath. ²Be gracious to me, O LORD, for I am languishing; O LORD, heal me, for my bones are shaking with terror. ³My soul also is struck with terror, while you, O LORD— how long? ⁴Turn, O LORD, save my life; deliver me for the sake of your steadfast love. ⁵For in death there is no remembrance of you; in Sheol (the place of the dead) who can give you praise? ⁶I am weary with my moaning; every night I flood my bed with tears; I drench my couch with my weeping. ⁷My eyes waste away because of grief; they grow weak because of all my foes. ⁸Depart from me, all you workers of evil, for the LORD has heard the sound of my weeping. ⁹The LORD has heard my supplication; the LORD accepts my prayer.

On the Way...

"O Lord—how long?" This is such a profound question. One that so many of us think but rarely verbalize. Maybe it's because we're afraid of offending or disappointing the Lord. Afraid that by speaking the question of our heart, we might inadvertently indicate that we've lost our way. Maybe we don't speak this question aloud because we're afraid that someone might think that we've given up hope or lost our faith.

I'm thankful for the psalmist who was courageous enough to cry out to the Lord with honesty and vulnerability. His courage can give rise to our courage. His vulnerably can give us the boldness we need to honestly name the pain in our own hearts.

This powerful psalm specifically names the ways that we hurt, the pain we feel when we languish, when we suffer. By painting a vivid picture, we see the psalmist on his bed and on his couch. We see the redness in his eyes from the excessive crying. We can touch the wetness on his sheets from the flood of tears. We hear the sound of his weeping. We feel the shaking of his bones as he waits in terror.

Can you see yourself in this psalm, beloved? Are you curled up on your couch or in your bed drenched in tears? Are your bones shaking in terror? Are you weary from all your moaning? Are you crying out, "O God—how long?"

You are in good company. The psalmist cried out to Lord, and you can do the same. This honest vulnerability is a gift that the psalmist gives to you.

In addition to the detail of the psalmist's pain, the psalm also includes a beautiful prayer: "[2]Be gracious to me O, Lord. [4]Turn, O LORD, save my life; deliver me for the sake of your steadfast love."

Clinging to the graciousness of the Lord who is the savior and deliverer, the psalmist calls on the mercy, the steadfast love, of the Lord. The good news is that the Lord heard the cry of the psalmist, heard his supplication, and received his prayer.

Rest assured, beloved, that the Lord hears your cry. The Lord sees your pain, your struggle. The Lord is present with you, holding on to you when you are shaking with terror, drying your tears, hearing your moaning. In the same way that the Lord heard the cry, the prayer of the psalmist, the Lord hears your prayer. The Lord hears your plea for help, your plea for deliverance from all that is burdening you. The Lord hears you and receives your prayer.

On the Way...

We're not told how the prayer of the psalmist is answered. And we don't know how your prayer will be answered either. That is the part of faith that remains a mystery. What we do know, and what the psalm confirms, is that the Lord listens we when cry out in prayer. The Lord receives our prayer. From there we fall into the gracious and steadfast love of Lord, who is our savior and deliverer.

Gracious God,

Receive my prayer. Hear the cries of my heart as I languish in the struggles of these days. Dry my tears and pull me close to you as you restore my soul, for you are my rock and my redeemer. Amen.

Reflection on Psalm 23

The Lord is my shepherd; I shall not want.
² He maketh me to lie down in green pastures:
he leadeth me beside the still waters.
³ He restoreth my soul: he leadeth me in the
paths of righteousness for his name's sake.
⁴ Yea, though I walk through the valley of the
shadow of death, I will fear no evil: for thou art
with me; thy rod and thy staff they comfort me.
⁵ Thou preparest a table before me in the presence
of mine enemies: thou anointest my head
with oil; my cup runneth over.
⁶ Surely goodness and mercy shall follow me all the
days of my life: and I will dwell in the house of the
Lord forever. (King James Version)

On the Way...

I suspect that you have this psalm memorized, that you can recall it, in your most favorite form.

One day I visited with an older lady at the hospital. She was alone and unresponsive in a darkened room. While sitting by her bedside, holding her hand, I started to pray for her and then read this psalm. She stirred a little bit and when I finished my prayer, she squeezed my hand. I asked her if she want to hear the psalm again and she squeezed my hand again. So, I read it again and again. Each time I finished she'd squeeze my hand indicating that she wanted to hear it one more time.

And some point, I noticed that her lips were moving at the same pace as I was speaking. I leaned in close and heard her saying the words with me. Eventually, she stopped speaking and didn't squeeze my hand again, so I stopped reciting the psalm. Once it was clear that she was sleeping I left her room. When I went back the next day to check on her, the nurse told me that she had died peacefully in the night.

There is no doubt that this psalm brings comfort in the face of hardship and death. it can also give comfort and reassure us in Life.

Life with a capital "L," *real* Life in tough times, *abundant* Life in the midst of fear and danger, Life in the very heart of God.

This psalm describes the very personal and intimate relationship between the shepherd and the sheep, between the creator and the created.

It's a relationship characterized by presence, provision, protection, and promise

<u>Presence</u>. At the center of this psalm is the phrase—"for you are with me." The Lord's relationship with us is all about presence.

Relationships are always about presence. When we are away from someone's presence, we feel separated, disconnected. And when we are in each other's presence again, we feel a sense of connection.

By the Lord's presence, you know that the Lord is interested in you, wanting only the best for you.

Without the shepherd's presence, the sheep would wander off to wherever sheep go—they'd get stuck, they'd be in danger.

Without the shepherd's presence, you too, would get lost in the darkest valleys and lose your way.

On the Way . . .

From the shepherd's presence, the Lord's presence in your life, flows everything else.

That's what **provision** is all about—Because the Lord is your shepherd, you receive all that you need to live—rest and nurture, restoration and guidance.

These are things that you need to live fully in the relationship that the Shepherd has established for and with you.

Without rest in green pastures, you will become exhausted, disconnected.

Without nurture beside still waters, you will become so dry that your body and mind will cease to function.

Without restoration of your soul, your trust in the shepherd will diminish.

Without guidance, you will wander aimlessly, seeking your own pleasure, your own needs, apart from the shepherd.

And so, the Lord provides for the sheep, for you, at every turn and in every way—sustaining the relationship that the Lord has created.

Presence, provision, and now **protection**—

The psalmist declares with all boldness—"Even though I walk through the valley of death, **I fear no evil**."

The psalmist acknowledges that evil is a part of life, that life is hard and scary, filled with uncertainty and suffering.

We all know that the valley of death or the darkest valley (as the New Revised Standard version translates this phrase) exists—that times are tough, that people struggle to make ends meet, that there is illness and death around us.

The psalmist proclaims the certainty of the Shepherd's presence in the midst of this valley.

"Even though I walk through the darkest valley, I fear no evil. For YOU are with Me.

This is the good news—you don't face these hardships alone. You are not alone in any of it. Claim this promise with these words:

Because the Lord is with me, I can face death, I can face illness.

Because the Lord is with me, I can grieve.

On the Way...

Because the Lord is with me, I can face my deepest pain.

Because the Lord is with me, I can love who I am.

Because the Lord is with me, I can know healing and wholeness.

Because the Lord is with me, when I am weak, then I am strong.

Because the Lord is with me, I can stop running and striving, hurrying and worrying.

Because the Lord is with me, I can know the peace that passes understanding.

Because the Lord is with me, I can rejoice in the Lord's salvation.

Because the Lord is with me, I can rejoice with those who rejoice and weep with those who weep.

Because the Lord is with me, I can celebrate the feast that is set before me every day.

Because the Lord is with me, I can let goodness and mercy actually catch me.

Because the Lord is with me, I can love others.

Pam Northrup

Because the Lord is with me, I can let others love me.

Because the Lord is with me, I can live as if I believe it, even though I am full of doubt, even though I don't always feel it, even though I'm afraid of what will happen, even though I am weary, even though I feel alone.

For you, Lord, are with me.

Beloved, you don't travel the valley of death or the darkest valleys alone. The Lord's presence, and the Lord's provision, and the Lord's protection are with you always.

This is the **<u>promise</u>** the Lord makes to you, to your love one, and to all of creation today.

Your Shepherd prepares a table for you—anoints your head with oil, and your cup overflows—because in the Lord's presence there is goodness and mercy. In the Lord's presence—you can live in hope, you can live in joy.

Because the Lord is with you.

Love is with you.

On the Way . . .

Peace and mercy and goodness are pursuing you, and you, Beloved, will dwell in the heart of the Lord now and forever.

Ever present God,

Thank you for the ways that you are present in my life. Thank you for providing me with what I need and for protecting me as I journey through this time. Hold me in the promise of your love this day and every day. Amen.

Reflection on Psalm 95:1-7

---

*¹O come, let us sing to the LORD;
let us make a joyful noise to the rock of our
salvation! ²Let us come into his presence with
thanksgiving; let us make a joyful noise to him with
songs of praise! ³For the LORD is a great God, and
a great King above all gods. ⁴In his hand are the
depths of the earth; the heights of the mountains are
his also. ⁵The sea is his, for he made it, and the dry
land, which his hands have formed. ⁶O come, let us
worship and bow down, let us kneel before the
LORD, our Maker! ⁷For he is our God,
and we are the people of his pasture,
and the sheep of his hand.*

We're called to worship God. To come into God's presence, not with downtrodden faces, not with silence and solemnity. We're called to sing, to make a joyful noise, to give thanks for all that God has made.

The idea of making a "joyful noise" always made Mom laugh. She loved music, loved singing, but never felt like she was very good at it. But that didn't stop her from making music. She'd say, "the Bible says to make a joyful noise, it doesn't say you have to be good at it!" So, praise God she did. And when she didn't have the strength to sing, we sang for her and to her.

Sitting at the beach with Mom, she often made reference to the beauty of creation. She marveled at the power of the ocean and at the creative nature of God, who made the smallest sand flea and the largest creature in the depths of the sea. Sitting at the beach was when Mom felt closest to God.

This psalm is a call to worship the Lord who is a great God and a great King above all gods. It is this God, our God, who made the earth and all there is, who made the mountains, the sea, and the dry land. All of this belongs to God, because God made it.

Just as God made the earth, mountains, sea, and dry land, God made us! We are part of God's good creation. When you look upon the tallest mountains, out across the widest oceans, and the vastness of the dry land, know that the same hand who created all that you see also created you! Remembering God as the creator connects us to the greatness of God as the ongoing action of creation continues.

Thankfully, the psalm also names God as the Shepherd. In this way we move from the bigness of God to the closeness of God. The shepherd holds the sheep in love, protects the sheep from the dangers that come their way. He provides food, water, and shelter, all that the sheep needs to survive. The shepherd gathers the sheep in the pasture and embraces them in his hand.

Jesus also talks about being the Shepherd. Jesus says in the Gospel of John, the 10th chapter: "^{14}I am the good shepherd. I know my own and my own know me, ^{15}just as the Father knows me and I know the Father. And I lay down my life for the sheep. ^{16}I have other sheep that do not belong to this fold. I must bring them also, and they will listen to my voice. So, there will be one flock, one shepherd."

Beloved, you are a sheep in the sheepfold of God. You are known and loved. The same God who created all there is also created you. This same God is your shepherd who pursues you when you wander

On the Way...

into dark and scary places. Your shepherd rescues you from the things that threaten you. Your shepherd holds you in love this day, and forever more.

Shepherding God,

I give you thanks for the beauty of all that you have made. I thank you for forming, naming, and claiming me as a sheep in your sheepfold. Hold me tight, dear Lord, as I journey through these days. Keep me safe from harm and draw me closer to your love. Amen.

Reflection on Psalm 139:1-14

---

¹O LORD, you have searched me and known me.
²You know when I sit down and when I rise up;
you discern my thoughts from far away.
³You search out my path and my lying down,
and are acquainted with all my ways.
⁴Even before a word is on my tongue,
O LORD, you know it completely.
⁵You hem me in, behind and before,
and lay your hand upon me.
⁶Such knowledge is too wonderful for me;
it is so high that I cannot attain it.
⁷Where can I go from your spirit?
Or where can I flee from your presence?
⁸If I ascend to heaven, you are there;
if I make my bed in Sheol, you are there.
⁹If I take the wings of the morning and
settle at the farthest limits of the sea,
¹⁰even there your hand shall lead me,
and your right hand shall hold me fast.

On the Way...

¹¹If I say, "Surely the darkness shall cover me, and the light around me become night,"
¹²even the darkness is not dark to you; the night is as bright as the day, for darkness is as light to you.
¹³For it was you who formed my inward parts; you knit me together in my mother's womb.
¹⁴I praise you, for I am fearfully and wonderfully made.

Caring for a loved one is exhausting and overwhelming work. It's easy to become focused on your loved one at the expense of other relationships. Your relationship with yourself, friends, coworkers, and even your relationship with God can suffer. The great beauty of this psalm is its assurance that the Lord's closeness to you is not dependent on your closeness to God.

Beloved, you are completely known by the Lord. And because the Lord knows you, you are never alone! In the middle of the night, when you're up caring for your loved one, the Lord is present with you. When you're feeling overwhelmed by all that's expected of you, the Lord is present with you. When you're asked to do something that makes you uncomfortable, the Lord is present with you.

This presence of the Lord protects you by hemming you in, behind and before. This hedge of protection surrounds you on all sides. When you're faced with tough decisions that cause you anxiety, the Lord brings clarity. When you're feeling threatened by things that are outside of your control, the Lord leads you. When you're tired and unable to sleep, the Lord holds you close.

The presence and protection of the Lord is upon you because the right hand of the Lord holds us fast. No matter where you go or what you do, the Lord protects you. When you drift away from God, God is still there. When you push God away, God is still there. When you forget about God, God is still there. The truth is that nothing you do or don't do will cause God to abandon you.

Sometimes it may be difficult to see God at work in your circumstances. It may be a challenge to know of God's protection. Things are hard. Your loved one is moving closer and closer to their death. God's presence and God's protection won't stop that from happening. When you want to see God at work, take a look at the little things: the tender care provided by

On the Way...

the hospice aide, a visit from a friend, a few minutes to take a walk outside, and the delivery of a meal. In each of these moments, God is at work bringing peace and mercy into your situation.

Beloved, the God who is present with you, who protects you, and who will not abandon you, is the same God who formed you. This God, our God, knit you together in your mother's womb. This is how God knows you completely. Nothing about you is hidden from God because God created you. And because God created you and your loved one, God is completely devoted to being present with you, demonstrating unconditional love to you today and every day.

Like the psalmist, the only thing that you can do now is to give thanks and praise to God.

Creator God,

Thank you for the ways that you intervene in my life and in the lives of those I love. Thank you for protecting me when things are hard. Thank you for being present with me when things are complicated. Please continue to hold me tightly as I journey through this time. I praise you for the many blessings you provide through the loving actions of others. Amen.

Reflection on Romans 5:6-11

⁶For while we were still weak, at the right time Christ died for the ungodly. ⁷Indeed, rarely will anyone die for a righteous person—though perhaps for a good person someone might actually dare to die. ⁸But God proves his love for us in that while we still were sinners Christ died for us. ⁹Much more surely then, now that we have been justified by his blood, will we be saved through him from the wrath of God. ¹⁰For if while we were enemies, we were reconciled to God through the death of his Son, much more surely, having been reconciled, will we be saved by his life. ¹¹But more than that, we even boast in God through our Lord Jesus Christ, through whom we have now received reconciliation.

Even the most faithful person has doubts. We've been taught that something which sounds too

On the Way...

good to be true probably is. We're suspicious and anticipate a loophole. The same is true with the promises of God.

So often we simply can't wrap our heads and our hearts around the enormity of God's love. A love based on what God does for us rather than what we do for God. That was bothering my Mom the day we talked about death and dying.

"Tell me it's not all a lie," she said.

I asked, "What do you mean, Mom?"

"Tell me," Mom continued, "that everything I've heard and believed about God is not a lie."

God's love for us and the extent that God goes to show that love is incomprehensible because it is so much bigger, so much wider then we can ever imagine. God's mercy is wider than the furthest limits of the galaxies and deeper than the deepest parts of the oceans. Because it's so big, it's challenging for you and me to grasp it, so we need to be reminded. We need to hear someone tell us again and again how much God loves us.

Beloved, God's action happened on your behalf while you were still "weak," "enemies," and "sinners." God doesn't wait for you to have an iron clad faith or a perfectly lived life. God acts in the death of Jesus. This is how God proves gracious love for you.

You need to look no further than the cross and the empty tomb to know of God's love for you. This love, God's love, is what brings reconciliation, a reconciliation that draws you to God, rather than away from God. Reconciliation that restores a relationship, rather than destroying it. Reconciliation that gives life, abundant and eternal life, rather than condemnation.

Live in that reconciliation today. Let the love of God, which loved you while you were at your lowest moment, embrace you today.

Loving God,

Embrace me today with your loving mercy. Quiet my anxious thoughts and calm my fears. Hold me close in your reconciling love today and forevermore. Amen.

Reflection on Romans 8:31-35, 37-39

---

³¹What then are we to say about these things? If God is for us, who is against us? ³²He who did not withhold his own Son, but gave him up for all of us, will he not with him also give us everything else? ³³Who will bring any charge against God's elect? It is God who justifies. ³⁴Who is to condemn? It is Christ Jesus, who died, yes, who was raised, who is at the right hand of God, who indeed intercedes for us. ³⁵Who will separate us from the love of Christ? Will hardship, or distress, or persecution, or famine, or nakedness, or peril, or sword?

³⁷No, in all these things we are more than conquerors through him who loved us. ³⁸For I am convinced that neither death, nor life, nor angels, nor rulers, nor things present, nor things to come, nor powers, ³⁹nor height, nor depth, nor anything else in all creation, will be able to separate us from the love of God in Christ Jesus our Lord.

On the Way...

Nothing! Nothing separates us from the love of God in Christ Jesus our Lord. Nothing!

This amazing promise is central to an understanding of God's grace, God's unconditional love.

Hardship, distress, persecution, famine, nakedness, peril, or sword have the potential to separate us from God. They are all-consuming. They turn our eyes inward, toward ourselves rather than outward, towards God.

Paul names these specific things to make it clear that the unconditional love of God overcomes every possible obstacle, every possible aspect of our human existence, every possible force that attempts to separate us from God.

Death, the end of our physical life, doesn't separate us.

Life, everything that happens to us as human beings, doesn't separate us.

Angels, heavenly beings, don't separate us.

Rulers, things that have power over us, don't separate us.

Not what happened in the past.

Pam Northrup

Not what's happening right now.

Not what will happen in the future.

None of these things, ***nothing***, separates us from the love of God in our Christ Jesus, our Lord.

Let this sink in for a minute. Give yourself time to wrap your head and your heart around the magnitude of God's love that is being described here.

When hardships, troubles, struggles, and difficulties of any kind are overwhelming you, know that they will not separate you from the love of God.

When distress, anxiety, suffering, and pain is challenging you, know that it will not separate you from the love of God.

When persecution, hostility, bullying, and oppression are happening to you, know that it will not separate you from the love of God.

Not scarcity or deficiency, not helplessness or vulnerability, not adversity or danger, not conflict or rebellion. Nothing will separate you from the love of God.

God is merciful and kind, slow to anger, and abounding in steadfast love. This is the very nature of

On the Way . . .

who God is. God's unconditional love lets nothing come between you and the One who created, claimed, and justified you. This unconditional love of God is fulfilled for you in the life, death, and resurrection of Jesus.

Beloved, in those moments when you doubt God's love for you, when you wonder if you're good enough, know that because of Jesus, you are a child of God and nothing will separate you from that love. Rest securely in this amazing grace.

Gracious God,

Thank you for your amazing and unconditional love that encompasses all that I am and all that my life is about. Strengthen my faith when doubts creep in that cause me to question your love. Hold me close in that love today and every day. Amen.

EPILOGUE

Traveling with Mom while she was dying in hospice care was a holy and precious time. I am thankful that we had that time together. She and I shared many heartwarming and poignant conversations and beautiful moments over the last two months of her life.

Sharing the journey with Bob and Jenny and the rest of the family was a gift. Thankfully, we managed the dynamics of our relationships and the stress of what we were doing in ways that deepened our relationships with each other. We moved through the days with intentionality and care. There were so many things that needed our attention which made it hard to keep everything on track. This was made even more challenging when sadness and exhaustion were part of the mix.

Thankfully, we worked together well. We gave one another space as we needed to. We pitched in to help wherever we could. We extended understanding, patience, and compassion to each other, knowing that

On the Way...

we were coping the best way that we knew how. In all these things, we grounded ourselves in the love that Mom had for each of us and in our love for each other. We saw this as a way to honor and celebrate Mom's life.

When I ask the WIGIAT (Where is God in all this) question, I am reminded of the many ways that God was present during our time with Mom. God was there steadying my hands when I needed to provide nursing care. God was there providing words of comfort and assurance to me and through me so that Mom experienced moments of peace. God was there through the care provided by members of the Interdisciplinary team every day. I've learned that when you expect God to be present, you are more likely to recognize that presence through the interactions and events of each day.

Our care for Mom was supplemented, no, extended, by the loving support of so many friends and other family members. Each of them interacted with Mom in ways that were life-giving. They gave selflessly of their time and energies because they loved Mom and they loved us. I am thankful for these people who were witnesses of God's love. Their involvement in her care was another way that God was present in all this.

There is nothing easy about caring for a loved one in the dying process. Both you and your loved one are saying "goodbye" a little bit every day. One day your loved one will be able to carry on a conversation and then another day, silence will be your companion. Some days, your loved one will have the energy to be up and about and then on other days, they will be confined to the bed. Your loved one might enjoy a favorite meal one day and then reject food and drink the next day. Visitors might be welcomed one day and turned away the next. As difficult as all this is to maneuver, it's normal.

Your loved one is making a transition from life in the here and now to the fulfillment of eternal life. Different people make this transition in different ways, and it's hard to predict what that will look like for your loved one. Know that in whatever way this plays out, it's okay. Its normal for your loved one. Saying good-bye and traveling through these transitions leads to grief for everyone.

Grief, a natural human response, manifests itself in different ways. Ways that may be affected by personality, culture, religion, and the nature of the relationship with the one who is dying. So often the words grief, mourning, and bereavement are used interchangeably. The truth is that they have different meanings.

Grief describes an individual's personal response to loss. It affects a person's emotional, physical, behavioral, cognitive, social and spiritual aspects of life. Mourning is the outward sign of grief. It shows itself in active and visible ways. Grief and mourning can begin as soon as the one you love receives a life-limiting diagnosis. Bereavement refers to grief and mourning that occur after death.

Grief that happens when someone dies without warning is sudden onset grief. With this kind of grief, there is no opportunity to talk about what matters most, no opportunity to enjoy favorite things together knowing that it's the last time, no opportunity for making apologies, or extending forgiveness, or proclaiming love. This is the grief I experienced after my father's death in 1983. Because of the things left unsaid and undone, this grief lingers today in a different kind of way.

Being "on the way" with someone who knows they are dying generates a progressive grief. In this kind of grief, you grieve a little bit each day along the way. You both know that everything you're doing is most likely the last time that you'll do it together. You have time to say what needs to be said and do what needs to be done. By the time Mom died, lots of words had been spoken and many tears had been shed.

This doesn't mean that we stopped grieving at Mom's death. Grief is never really finished. It just manifests itself differently. There are different models used to describe the task of grieving. One of the oldest and maybe most familiar is the Five-Stage Model of denial, anger, bargaining, depression, and acceptance established by Dr. Elisabeth Kübler-Ross.[2] Another widely accepted model is defined by J. William Worden. He identifies the Four Tasks of Mourning. These tasks include: 1) accept the reality of loss; 2) process the pain of grief; 3) adjust to the world without the deceased; and 4) find a way to remember.[3]

---

2 Elisabeth Kubler-Ross, M.D., "On Death & Dying: What the dying have to teach doctors, nurses, clergy, and their families." (New York: Simon & Schuster, 1969).

3 William J. Worden, "Grief Counseling & Grief Therapy, Fifth Edition: A Handbook for the Mental Health Professional." (New York: Springer Publishing Company, LLC, 2018).

On the Way...

Each of these models, and many others, seek to make sense of a process that is extremely complex. They may help those who are grieving find comfort in knowing that others have shared similar experiences. They offer a framework for the emotional, mental, spiritual, and physical experience of grieving the death of a loved one which might make sense of what's happening and how they're feeling. A limitation to models that try to capture the complexity of grief is that they may inadvertently present grieving in a linear fashion. They set an expectation that a person's grief will move through each stage, each task, in a predictable way.

This has not been my experience with grief. For me, grief is more like a roller coaster. There are times when my grief is intense, nearly unbearable—like being at the top of the roller coaster, when your heart is racing, and you can't catch your breath, while you wait to go down the steep decline. Other times, I'm rolling along in the low places and my grief is manageable, less consuming, less overwhelming. As I ride the roller coaster, I am moving in and out of the intensity of grief. This ride never stops, it slows down and speeds up from time to time, especially around birthdays, anniversaries, holidays, and at other moments when I wish that mom was still with us.

Over the last 35 years since the death of my Dad and the last 10 years since Mom died, I have learned to live with my grief, with the hole in my heart that comes at the death of those you love. I don't expect this hole to heal and I don't think I want it to. For me, this hole is the place where my love for my parents continues to live. My focus now is on honoring and remembering them as I go on living.

Being "on the way" with Mom as she got closer and closer to death was a blessing and a privilege. While I still grieve her death, my heart is filled with contentment because we cared for her to the very best of our abilities. This holy and precious time continues to shape my life in ways that I am still discovering.

As you are "on the way" with your loved one and those who are journeying with you, my hope is that the stories and biblical reflections included in this collection have provided opportunities for you to laugh, ponder, cry, and share your own stories with each other. Maybe you've seen yourself or your loved one in one of these stories. Maybe one of the biblical reflections has brought you comfort as you rested in the presence of God. Maybe together they have given you a sense of peace in the midst of a most difficult, most holy, most precious time.

On the Way...

Comforting God,

Thank you for traveling with us through this difficult and holy time. Thank you for the gift of (insert the name of your loved one), for the ways that her/his life touches our lives. Sustain us now as we persevere along the road that leads from life, through death, to eternal life. Grant us what we need in each moment as we are on the way together. Amen.

The Lord bless you and keep you. The Lord make his face shine on you and be gracious to you. The Lord look upon you with favor and give you peace.

Appreciation

I express deep appreciation to:

Bob, my husband, for willingly and lovingly sharing in the task of caring for my Mom; for encouraging me to write and complete this book; and for holding me in love as I continue to grieve.

Jenny, my sister, for the love we've shared throughout our lives which enabled us to care for Mom; for exciting sister trips; for her support of this book; and for our ongoing friendship.

Hazel's granddaughters: Amanda, Becky, Jessie, Abi, and Maggie for providing care to Grammy and continuing to hold her in love.

My daughters, Amanda and Becky, and my daughter-in-law, Ashley for their encouragement and support in writing this book and for reading the early drafts and providing feedback.

Heidi Kliene, my personal coach, for her words of affirmation and encouragement and for holding me accountable to my goals and plans that brought this book to completion.

The Rev. Dr. Tony Everett, my professor for pastoral care at Lutheran Theological Southern Seminary, for teaching me a framework for providing pastoral care and writing the Forward for this book.

Kevin Coppolino, the cover designer, Jennifer Bateman, the book editor; and Jennifer Henderson, the book formatter. Their expertise helped to bring this book to completion.

Gary Williams, my coach through the Self-Publishing School, for his encouragement and wisdom along the way.

The nurses, aides, and social workers at Duke Homecare & Hospice for providing compassionate care to my mom and our family.

The many friends who supported us in our caregiving and who loved and cared for Hazel through their companionship.

The faith community at Good Shepherd Lutheran Church, Raleigh, NC who continue to hold Mom in their hearts as evidenced by her picture in the kitchen where she loved to serve.

Rev. Scott Homesley, my colleague and friend, who provided pastoral care to me and created the space for me to be away from pastoral ministry to care for my Mom.

My colleagues and the parishioners at Our Saviour Lutheran Church, Southern Pines, NC; St. Mark by the Sea Lutheran Church, Palm Coast, FL; and St. Philip Lutheran Church, Raleigh, NC who cared for me in my grief and who allowed me to care for them in theirs.

Each one of these individuals and communities are deeply important to me and I thank God for them and their presence in my life.

For More Information about Hospice

The Hospice Foundation.
https://hospicefoundation.org.

National Hospice Foundation.
https://www.nationalhospicefoundation.org

Medicare Hospice Benefits.
https://www.medicare.gov/Pubs/pdf/02154-Medicare-Hospice-Benefits.PDF

National Hospice and Palliative Care Organization.
https://www.nhpco.org

About the Author

Pam Northrup is a hospice chaplain and a graduate of Lutheran Theological Southern Seminary. She was ordained in the Evangelical Lutheran Church in America (ELCA) in 2006. She's served as pastor at Our Saviour Lutheran Church, Southern Pines, NC; St. Mark by the Sea Lutheran Church, Palm Coast, FL; and St. Philip Lutheran Church, Raleigh, NC. As a trained Stephen Leader, she has prepared countless lay people to serve as Stephen Ministers who provide confidential Christian caregiving to people in need.

On the Way...

Her passion in ministry is journeying with people as they face the ups and downs of life. She sees the movement from life, through death, to eternal life as the holiest moment in a person's life. Her passion in life is spending time with friends and family, especially her grandchildren. She enjoys playing board games, assembling puzzles, making music, coloring, and making art collages.

Pam is recognized as an outstanding preacher, gifted teacher, compassionate listener, and skilled facilitator. Pam is proud to identify herself as an Army Brat. She believes that this experience, her vocation as a parent, and her work as a special education teacher, Girl Scout professional, adult educator, and pastor influence the way she makes sense of the world.

Pam lives in Knightdale, NC with her husband, Bob, and their two dogs. You can read a collection of her sermons and blog posts and learn more about her at www.onthewayliving.org.

Contact her at pam@onthewayliving.org if you'd like to talk about speaking and teaching opportunities.

www.ingramcontent.com/pod-product-compliance
Lightning Source LLC
Chambersburg PA
CBHW022215090526
44584CB00012BB/556